The Book

Other Books by Lewis Turco

The Green Maces of Autumn, Voices in an Old Maine House, 2002

A Book of Fears: Poems, with Italian translations by Joseph Alessia, 1998

Bordello: A Portfolio of Poems and Prints, with George O'Connell, 1996

Emily Dickinson, Woman of Letters: Poems and Centos from Lines in Emily Dickinson's Letters, 1993

The Shifting Web: New and Selected Poems, 1989

The Fog: A Chamber Opera in One Act, with Walter Hekster, 1987

The Compleat Melancholick, Being a Sequence of Found, Composite, and Composed Poems Based Largely upon Robert Burton's The Anatomy of Melancholy, 1985

American Still Lifes, 1981

Pocoangelini: A Fantography & Other Poems, 1971

The Inhabitant, 1970

Awaken, Bells Falling: Poems 1959–1967, 1968

First Poems, 1960

The Book of Forms, Third Edition, 2000

The Book of Literary Terms, 1999

Shaking the Family Tree, A Remembrance, 1998

The Public Poet, 1991

The New Book of Forms, 1986

Visions and Revisions of American Poetry, 1986

Poetry: An Introduction Through Writing, 1973

The Book of Forms: A Handbook of Poetics, 1968

Lewis Turco

THE BOOK OF DIALOGUE

How to Write Effective
Conversation in Fiction,
Screenplays, Drama, and Poetry

University Press of New England
Hanover and London

University Press of New England, 37 Lafayette St., Lebanon, NH 03766

© 1989, 2004 by Lewis Turco

Original cloth edition published in 1989 by Writer's Digest Books

First University Press of New England paperback edition 2004

Library of Congress Cataloging-in-Publication Data

Turco, Lewis.
The book of dialogue : how to write effective conversation in fiction,
screenplays, drama, and poetry / Lewis Turco.
    p.   cm.
ISBN 1–58465–361–2 (pbk. : alk. paper)
1. Dialogue. 2. Fiction—Authorship. 3. Motion picture authorship.
4. Playwriting. 5. Poetry—Authorship. I. Title.
PN1551.T85 2004
808.3'96—dc22   2003023754

ACKNOWLEDGMENTS

"Bordello" was published as a limited edition portfolio of PoemPrints,
poems by Lewis Turco, prints by George O'Connell, Oswego: Grey Heron/
Mathom, and is reprinted here by permission of the author. © 1971, 1996,
2004 by Lewis Turco, all rights reserved.

"The Man in the Booth" by Lewis Turco originally appeared in *Plough-
shares,* x:2–3, 1984.

"The Museum of Ordinary People" first appeared in the anthology
American Fiction 2, edited by Michael C. White & Alan Davis, New York:
Birch Lane Press, 1991.

"An Old-Fashioned Kind of Guy" was published in *New Times,* No. 678,
March 21, 1984, and is reprinted here by permission of the author © 1984,
2004 by Lewis Turco, all rights reserved.

(Continued on page 184)

For my sweethearts,
Jean, Melora, Jessima,
and, as of 12 September 2003,
Phoebe Louise.

Contents

The Book of Dialogue

Introduction

Several months elapsed between my being commissioned to write this book on the art and craft of writing dialogue in fiction and my actually sitting down to begin work on the typescript. That's not to say nothing was happening. I'd written the outline of the book, so I knew generally what it was I had to say—my first problem had to do with *how* to say it. That's always a major problem with writing anything. *How* to say something is more than half the battle. It takes some thought to decide on approach and tactics.

So I was doing a lot of thinking. At last I had a brainstorm—it was simplicity itself. I would write a book about dialogue in the form of a dialogue.

There's nothing new about the method of what's called the "Socratic dialogue." It has been around for a millennium and a half, and it's a sound teaching technique. It was invented by Plato. Many people who read Plato's dialogues believe that they are a sort of verbatim transcript of what Socrates said as he walked about the grounds of his "Academy," the Athenian agora, around 400 B.C., as though Plato were a kind of human tape recorder who listened carefully to the great philosopher-teacher and took excellent notes that he passed on to posterity, but that is far from the case. In fact, the *Dialogues* were works of fiction.

"For Plato has a numerous repertory of *dramatis personae*," says the classic eleventh edition of *The Encyclopedia Britannica* (in Vol. 21, p. 811), "who stand in various relations to his chief character"—that is, Socrates—including "the impetuous Chaerephon,

Apollodorus the inseparable weak brother, old Crito the true-hearted, Phaedo the beloved disciple, Simmias and Cebes," and so on and so forth. "Parmenides with his magnificent depth is made to converse with the imaginary Socrates who is still quite young."

"*Made to converse* with the *imaginary* Socrates." Clearly, Plato's *Dialogues* are works of fiction at the same time that they are works of nonfiction. They are philosophical textbooks that tell a story, but their chief purpose is to discuss the nature of truth as it applies to various disciplines: ethics, politics, law, logic, science, religion. There is a paradox built into the system of the dialogues: Plato wrote lies in order to tell the truth. That's what fictioneers and playwrights do and have always done. Plato was not only an early and great philosopher of the Western world, he was an early fiction writer as well.

Where did Plato (c. 427–347 B.C.) get the idea for his dialogues? If we look at Greek classical literature we find two types of narrative that are older than or roughly contemporary with Plato's *Dialogues*—the epics of Homer (c. ante-700 B.C.), and the plays of Aristophanes (c. 448–388 B.C.) and Euripides (c. 480–406 B.C.). The epic was the first novel, the most obvious difference between the two being the mode of writing; that is to say, the classical epic was written in verse (metered language), and the modern novel is written in prose (unmetered language). There are other differences, of course, but they don't concern us here. However, drama does concern us as the source of dialogue, so we will spend time in the course of future pages talking about the difference between dialogue as it appears in fiction and in drama.

What is my role in the evolution of Plato's invention? Simply that my subject in this book is dialogue itself. I'll use the Socratic dialogue to teach dialogue writing. I'll make up my own version of a Platonic fictional character in order to discuss the writing of dialogue in fiction while writing a piece of nonfiction fiction in the process!

Are there any advantages to this method?

Yes, there are. For one thing, I can set up a tension between the "author" (who is himself, if truth were known, a fictive invention) and an "antagonist," just as a fiction writer does in writing a short story or a novel when he or she pits a protagonist against an antagonist—a hero against a villain, if you prefer. Another thing I can do is to illustrate as we go along, in the text itself, the methods, techniques, and conventions of dialogue writing.

Is there anything else that can be done?

Most certainly. I can develop the personality of my fictive foil, show how dialogue is a builder of character in a narrative. At the beginning of the book this unnamed dramatic "persona," to use the term of the *Britannica,* is nothing more than a disembodied voice. Within a few pages, if I do my job right, my character will begin to be a person, a stand-in for an aspect of the author, that facet which is a student rather than a teacher. I will be talking to myself and to the reader simultaneously, and it's possible that during the course of the book we may learn something about the art of writing dialogue in fiction.

Since the first edition of this book was published in 1989 as *Dialogue,* many things have happened to it. It has been translated into Italian by Sylvia Biasi and published in Italy by Editrice Nord of Milan in 1992; it has been published in paperback by Robinson of London in 1991 and later as part of another book by Robinson, *How to Write a Mi££ion, The Complete Guide to Becoming a Successful Author* in 1995, and the first American paperback edition appeared in 1999. I don't know how many printings it's gone through, but the original edition went through eight printings in those fourteen years, and the twenty-first century has ensued. Clearly, it is time for a new edition.

And this is it. It is basically the same book, but there are complete examples rather than partial ones, as often there were originally. The genre of poetry has been added to fiction, cinema, radio, and drama, a feature not found in other books on the subject. I hope the audience of this century finds *The Book of Dialogue* as useful as the audience of the last century did, and as do the audiences for its companion books, *The Book of Forms, A Handbook of Poetics* and *The Book of Literary Terms, The Genres of Fiction, Drama, Nonfiction, Literary Criticism and Scholarship.*

Lewis Turco
Emeritus Professor of English Writing Arts
Oswego State University
7 March 2003

Chapter 1

Definitions

Dialogue

Just exactly what *is* dialogue?

You're writing this book. Why don't you tell me?

I beg your pardon?

Why, what did you do?

Who are you?—if you don't mind my asking.

Well, since you're the author of this book, I guess I must be a character you've invented. Either that, or I'm a would-be writer who's been hanging around waiting for you to say something interesting.

What's your name?

I must have amnesia, because I don't think I have one. Why don't you give me one?

I'll think about it.

While you're doing that, can I ask you a question?

Sure. Go ahead.

Okay—what's dialogue?

Dialogue is a conversation.

Like what we're having right now?

Exactly.

If you already knew, why did you ask me?

I didn't ask you. I was just talking out loud. I didn't know you were there.

Oh, sure! sure! You expect me to believe that?

Well, I didn't know you were there *yet*.

You thought you were talking to yourself?

You've got it! I'm still not sure I'm not talking to myself.

Forms of Dialogue 1: Monologue and Soliloquy

What do you call talking to yourself? Can you have a conversation with yourself?

Of course. It's called a *soliloquy*. That is, it's called a soliloquy if you're not expecting any answer—in other words, if you're just expressing your thoughts aloud.

Give me an example.

Okay, if you'll leave the room.

Leave the room? How can you give me an example if I'm not around?

How can I give you an example if you are?

This is a real baffler.

Just leave the room. You can read the soliloquy afterwards.

All right, all right. Give me a second. . . .

Format and Punctuation 1

Are you gone? Is he gone? I heard the door close, so I guess he must be out of the room. Now, where was I? Oh, right—I was going to think out loud. Let's see. Who is this person I'm talking to? It appears he's a character I've invented for the purposes of this book. He needs a name, it seems to me, and I'd best begin using quotation marks for our speeches so that people can keep track of who's speaking:

"Well, people know who I am because my name's on the title page of the book, but they have no idea who my partner is. In fact, he's a 'foil,' a person who is used to further the purposes of another person, in this case, the Author. I'd best start another paragraph at this point because I'm going to change my focus. I won't close my quotes at the end of this paragraph, though, because I'm going to continue to speak.

"I will, however, start the paragraph with quotes so that when my foil gets back he'll know I'm still talking. What the hell, I think I'll just call him Fred. That's as good a name as any. I'll call him back now, and then I'll close the quotes on this soliloquy made of two paragraphs—hey, Fred! Come on back!"

Fred opens the door and sticks his head into the room. "Are you talking to me?" he asks.

"Yes."

He enters and closes the door behind him. "Since when is my name Fred?"

"Since two minutes ago."

"Oh. Well, it's not much of a name, but it's an improvement over nothing. Let's see what you've written. I need to check out what a soliloquy looks like." Fred bends over the Author's shoulder and squints at the video monitor of the computer. "Okay, pal, scroll it back so I can see the soliloquy."

Types of Fictional Characters: Personae

The author scrolls back along the file to the point in question and Fred reads for a moment, then stiffens. "A foil? I'm a foil? How come I'm not a protagonist, or at least an antagonist, like you said in the Introduction? Why do I have to be a foil instead of a character? That makes me a 'second banana,' right?"

The Author sighs—he can already see where this line of questioning is leading. Fred is beginning to be something of a pain and it can only get worse. The Author needs to regain control of his book. "You're a foil because I need one. I don't need a protagonist or an antagonist because this isn't going to be a story, it's a Socratic dialogue."

"I get the picture about the soliloquy, and I understand that a dialogue is a conversation, such as the one we're having at the moment, but what's a 'Socratic' dialogue?" Fred looks quizzically at the Author.

Uses of Italics

The Author sighs again. *Brother,* he thinks, *this is going to get complicated. All Fred knows how to do is ask questions.* Aloud, he says, "I thought you said you'd read the Introduction. Socrates was an ancient Greek philosopher who taught his pupils by means of conversation—questions and answers. Since this is a book on how to write dialogue, I figured the most appropriate way to proceed was by means of the Socratic dialogue. Go back and take another look at that Introduction. You missed a few things. Any more questions?"

"Lots." Fred gives the Author a big grin. His rather narrow features fold themselves into a lot of small wrinkles. His pale skin seems to be paper thin and very pliable. He has blue eyes, the Author notices for the first time, and rather sparse, almost colorless blonde hair. "I see you're using quotation marks now to help keep things tidy."

"And to allow me to put in descriptions and actions and things like that, so that the speeches can be immediately recognized as speeches."

"I like the way you used italics, too," Fred says, "to show unspoken thoughts, not a soliloquy. They don't do it that way in dramas, do they?"

Scripts

Author. No. Scripts look like this.

Fred. Yes, I see. And in between the speeches the playwright can insert stage directions and descriptions of setting and things like that, right?

(Fred moves across the set, stage right, sits down on a chair and crosses his legs.)

Author. Exactly. Plays aren't meant to be read except by the people staging them, so the script is laid out in this way for the benefit of the actors and the other personnel of the drama. The audience can see the actions, the scenes, and so forth. They can see who's speaking, so there's no need for quotation marks or descriptions of places, situations, people and actions, as there is in fiction.

(Fred uncrosses his legs and gets up again.) "You know," he says, "this is kind of interesting."

"How do you do that?" the Author asks.

"Do what?"

"Knit your brows."

"Don't ask me." Fred shrugs. "You're the author around here. I don't even know what 'knit' means."

Author. (aside) If you did, you'd be a knit-wit.

Fred. What did you say? I couldn't hear.

Author. You weren't supposed to. It was an *aside*.

Fred. What. . .

Author. (before Fred can continue) Don't ask. An aside is a remark made by a character intended to be heard only by the audience of a play, not the other characters onstage.

Fred. I see. Can you have an aside in fiction, too?

Forms of Dialogue 2: Asides

The Author sighs deeply. *"Can you have an aside in fiction, too?"* *he asks. Brother, this Fred character knows nothing at all!*

"What are you mumbling?" Fred scowls.

"Sure, you can have an aside in fiction. Usually it will be printed in italics and not put into quotation marks so that the reader can distinguish it from a monologue. But to answer your other question, 'knit' means scowling, I think, but never mind."

Fred makes an effort to stop scowling. "What's the biggest difference between a fiction writer and a playwright?" he asks.

Narration 1: Exposition

"The fiction writer isn't limited to one or two *writing* techniques; rather, he may choose from a wide range of narrative devices. The playwright, however, is limited to the *writing* techniques of dialogue, monologue, soliloquy or aside, though on occasion a play (such as *Our Town* by Thornton Wilder) may have a narrator on the stage filling in the audience on portions of the narrative that take place 'offstage'—between segments (acts or scenes)of the drama—or on background information that the audience may need in order to understand the significance of the dramatic segments."

"That's called 'exposition,' isn't it?"

"Right, Fred." The Author is impressed. "Now and again you surprise me. Exposition is a major consideration in the essay, and it's an important element of both fiction and drama. Exposition includes actions and situations that 'took place' before the story began but which led up to the actions of the story."

"Is that all exposition is? Past actions?"

"No. We'll talk about some of the other things later on, but for new it's enough to remember that usually, especially in drama, the exposition is worked into the fabric of the narrative by the characters of the story through reminiscence or conversation."

"That must be tough to do. What else can the fiction writer do that the dramatist can't?

Viewpoint 1: Subjective/Objective/Dramatic

"The fiction writer can get inside his or her characters' heads, show the reader what the personae are thinking. In other words, the fiction writer can have subjective *access* to characters. The playwright has only objective access, so he or she has to use soliloquies or asides in order to verbalize thoughts or feelings. The playwright might even have to have characters address the audience directly under certain circumstances."

"I see what you mean," Fred says, a faraway look in his eyes. The Author surmises that Fred is visualizing a play.

"Don't feel sorry for the playwright, though," the Author admonishes his foil. "Although it may at first glance seem that the dramatist is more limited than the fictionist, in fact that's not the case. In some ways he or she is less limited because a playwright can put characters into what appears, for instance, to be a real room. The fictionist would have to describe that room. And we see the characters physically in a play—their clothes, actions, coloring; we can hear the nuances of their voices. The fiction writer has to choose various descriptive techniques that would enable one to convey these things to the reader. The dramatist can simply get on with the narrative, which is the reason few plays utilize a narrator who can slow things down, and the essence of drama is action—*dramatic* action, and that's true for fiction as well."

"I'm beginning to catch on." Fred gets up and begins to pace the room. "Still, both the fictionist and the dramatist have the narrative in common, don't they?"

"Yes, indeed."

Fred stops and stares at the back of the head of the Author, who ignores him and goes on typing.

"Gosh, you're clever!" Fred says.

Diction 1: Fancy Words

The Author thinks he detects a bit of irony in Fred's voice, so he turns to look, but Fred's demeanor is impassive.

"My 'demeanor is impassive'? What kind of language is that?" Fred asks.

"You're right. It's a slip in the level of diction of this piece. I'll try not to do it again. . ." the Author holds up his hand when he sees Fred's mouth begin to open ". . . and we'll talk about diction later on."

"And you used 'admonishes' back there a ways, too."

The Author glares at his foil.

Forms of Dialogue 3: Monologue—an Example

"Okay, you can stop giving me the evil eye. You know what you haven't done?"

"What?"

"You *haven't* given me an example of a monologue."

"A monologue is half of a conversation. It's a speech to a character who's presumed to be present, though a listener may not be evident to the reader. Here's a whole story written in the form of a monologue."

"A *whole* story?" Fred sounds incredulous.

"Yes, and it's going to get us into, among other things, the question of narration—when is a narrator not a narrator? The speaker in this story is the mother of a severely retarded child. Her speech will characterize her and even give us background material—her class, her marital situation, her hopes and fears and desires."

"Are you trying to tell me," Fred asks shaking his head, his hair flopping down over his eyes, "that in this story speech is everything?"

The Author nods. "*Everything*. And not even all of a speech, just one side of the conversation. Now, imagine the speaker is standing in her kitchen doorway welcoming a neighbor who has just returned from vacation—by the way, Fred, we're not going to need quotation marks because the speech does not pass back and forth between characters":

Savants

Oh, hi, hon! Come on in! When did you and Harry get back? Come in and sit down—the coffee's all ready, see? A fresh pot on the stove. Funny I didn't hear your car come in next door last night. I must've been busy with Timmy—honestly, he's been driving me crazy lately. I wish he could hear, at least, so I could get through to him.

So tell me all about it—where'd you go on vacation? How long's it been, now? Only two weeks? Seems it's at least a month. I didn't have anybody to talk to. Jim's no company at all—he's either watching TV or at a bar, or out bowling with the guys or fishing—but I don't have to tell you. Lucky you! You had Harry all to yourself for two whole weeks! Oh, well, sure, to yourself and the kids. I bet they were out in the woods all the time while you stayed with the camper, right? Oh, sure, you *and* the girls. Still, I bet it was nice.

What'd I do? Not much, let me tell you. But you know, I saw something on TV the other night that just made my eyes open up like a can of cat food. Oh, ignore him, that's just Timmy again. I give up trying to figure out what ails him. Let him cry. It's all he does all the time anyway. I'm about at the end of my rope. Maybe Jim's right—it's probably time to put him in a home or something. I can't cope any more.

What was I saying? Oh, yeah, the TV. I was watching a rerun of "Sixty Minutes" the other night. We never watch that show, but we saw everything else that was on last fall, all reruns, so I watched it. Jim wasn't home, just me and Timmy. Honestly, hon, let me tell you, it was the most amazing thing I ever saw in my life—no, really, *the* most amazing. It was all about these retarded people, so of course, on account of Timmy, I was interested. But you never saw such retards in your life!

There was three of them, and they were special, because each one was a genius somehow, besides being dummies. Don't look at me like that! I'm telling you the truth. Write CBS if you don't believe me. They called them "idiot servants," or something like that. You heard of that? Really? Well, I never did.

The first one was really stupid-looking. He had this big moron grin, and his eyes looked empty—like Timmy's. But what he could do with his hands! See, he took wax—canning wax, it looked like, and he molded it into little statues of animals—horses mostly, but other things too. My eyes nearly fell out of my head! They were perfect—I mean, really perfect! Somehow, they took these perfect statues and made a mold out of them, I guess, and then poured metal into the mold and made statues, so he had help, but they were selling these things for hundreds of dollars! God, I wish Timmy could do something like that! Could we use the money.

So, anyway, when the announcer asked this dummy how he did it, he answered, "I 'member," and pointed at his head! And when the announcer asked how he could remember, he said, "I smart." Imagine that, "I Smart!" About as smart as a bedpost.

The next one wasn't as good—all he could do was remember dates. What's so great about that? Well, he could remember any date in the entire history of the world, and as far forward as you wanted to go! No, I don't mean he knew history, or what happened on a certain day, but I do mean the day of the week—Monday or Tuesday or whatever, and the date.

But if he was alive on a certain day, he could tell you the weather of that day! Besides having this little calculator in his head, he had a perfect memory! Excuse me just a sec, hon—I'm gonna go give Timmy a bottle and change his diapers so I can have a little peace. Imagine that, a bottle and diapers, and he's seven years old! It's like having a baby forever. I'll be right back.

There, that didn't take long, did it? He's quiet at last. What a relief. Look, I'm sweating under the arms and on my forehead, and it's barely seventy degrees in here.

So, anyway, he just sits there and answers these questions the announcer throws at him. But when he asks the dummy to multiply two times three, he can't do it! This retard looked more or less normal, not like the other one, with his mouth gaping open and slobbering down his chin. But still, not normal, you know what I mean? And when they ask him how come he can do all these things with dates, this one says he's smart, too! I had to laugh, or I would have if I wasn't so damn mad. Here I am, sitting there looking at these dummies on TV! On TV! Dummies! Jesus. I got to wondering who was dumber, them or me for watching them. God knows I ought to be an expert at it.

But it was the third one that was the most amazing of all. This one wasn't just a dummy! Oh, no. He was more like Timmy, only even worse. Not only was he a moron, but he was blind, too. Timmy's deaf, but it's close. But that's not all—he's retarded, he's blind, and he's got cerebral palsy! Born with it.

Now, you're not going to believe what I tell you, but it's true anyhow. I swear, it's the most amazing thing I ever saw in my life—saw with my own eyes, and heard with my own ears.

They interviewed the lady who took care of this vegetable, and that's just what he was at first, a vegetable. He just laid there on his bed, she said, and he didn't do anything. Not a thing. But one day this old lady—she's old now, I don't know how long she was taking care of the dummy—gets it into her head that if she buys a piano—a piano!—and puts it beside his bed, maybe something will happen.

What's the chances of that, do you suppose? I mean, chances of getting an idea like that, first of all, and then, second, something happening? Don't look at me like that! I'm not making this up. Call up CBS and ask them, or ask around the neighborhood—somebody else must've saw the show. So anyway, she buys this little piano and puts it beside this bed, and it sits there for I don't know how long.

Then, one night, when her and her husband are in bed, she wakes up because she hears this beautiful music coming from somewhere. So help me. Come on, don't look at me like that, I swear to God—cross my heart! She rolls over and she says to her hubby, "Did you leave the radio on?" "No," he says, so she gets up to see what's going on—I guess he does too—and they go trailing off up the hall to this vegetable's room, and they open the door and turn on the light—there he sits, on the edge of his bed, I guess, with these fingers all floppy on the keys, playing something. I don't mean one note at a time, either, I mean playing something like Liberace plays!

The rest of the show is about this idiot servant giving concerts. He even begins to talk, which he never used to do. And he says he can do these things because he's got a good mind, too. A good mind! Never had a lesson in his life, and he plays like Liberace. Oh, Jesus, I thought, wouldn't it be nice if Timmy could do something like that? Maybe it would be worth it, then, all the agony.

Don't touch me, okay? I'm sorry. I'll be all right. I'll just use a napkin. There. Well, anyhow, when Jim comes home, I tell him all about it. He's half in the bag, and he thinks *I've* been hitting the juice! At first he laughs, and then, when I keep on, he slugs me—gives me a slap that throws me half across the room! And I know I'm gonna have to do this all by myself.

Just wait, I'm getting there. I'll tell you what I did. The next day I left Timmy by himself in his crib for a couple hours—what's he going to do? He's not going anywhere. All he can do is cry, and if there's nobody around to hear him, then there's *nobody,* because he can't even hear himself. I took the bus down to the mall. I was just about to go into the music store to get Timmy a guitar or something—I know, I know, it was stupid—probably turning into a retard myself by now, but all I could think about was that damn piano. Anyway, like I said, I was just about to go into the music store when I realize what I'm doing and stop dead in my tracks.

"How's he going to hear to play a guitar?" I ask myself. "That's even worse than cerebral palsy." And I can't think of what to do at first. But then my eye happens to catch a sign across the hall—"Art Supplies," it says. It's a hobby store. That's when I get my bright idea. Maybe I'm a servant too. I go in, and I buy a little easel and some paper and some watercolors and brushes.

Well, I'll cut it short. I brought it all home and set it up beside Timmy's crib. I sat there for a while, showing him how to do it—making stick people and so on. No, it didn't work. It's still in there beside the crib—I keep hoping. I had to patch it together after Jim saw it and got mad, and I had to Scotch-tape some of the paper where it got torn, but it's still in there and nothing's happened. Nothing's going to happen, either, except. . . .

I can't tell you, but I got to tell somebody. Jim never looks into Timmy's room, but he finally did last night. He saw it and got mad and said he was tired of coming home and finding out that I been wasting his money again. And he was getting tired of coming home at all to that kid in there, that retarded squash laying around in a crib forever. Who needs it? Who needs a wife that all she can do is give a man a thing like that? And she won't even get rid of it, give it away to a hospital—no, all she can do is sit around and watch it drain money out of his wallet.

And then he beat me again—a good one this time—that's why I'm wearing these dark glasses for breakfast. Yeah, I know you knew, but now it's said I feel better. And I hope I'm going to feel better yet, but it's hard.

So when he's through with me, and he goes out again, I drag myself into Timmy's room, and I lift him up to his feet in the crib, and I hit him. Gimme that napkin. I beat him as hard as Jim beat me. No, you can't see him. I don't want you to see him. That was last night—that's why

Timmy's crying all the time this morning. Jim's not been home yet, not since he took off around midnight, and I'm afraid of what he's going to do when he sees the TV—that goddam TV, and all the glass laying around the living room floor.

Fred puts down the story and whistles softly. "That was a real *tour de force*," he says. "The whole thing was nothing but one person speaking."

"Actually, that sort of thing is done in poetry as well as in fiction. In poetry it's often called a *dramatic monologue*."

Fred nods. I've heard of it somewhere, haven't I? Didn't Robert Browning write some of those?"

"Right. One of them is titled 'Porphyria's Lover,' and you can find it in *The Book of Forms*. Another famous one is 'Sestina Altaforte' by Ezra Pound, written in the early twentieth century. But Edgar Lee Masters at about the same time wrote a whole book of them, *The Spoon River Anthology*."

"Wasn't that a bunch of dead people speaking from their graves?" Fred asked and then shivered.

"It was. And they were talking about each other, so that you got a lot of interplay among them—you might call it *interactive monologue*."

"Anyone else do something like that?" Fred asked.

"The first in the English language was probably Geoffrey Chaucer in the fourteenth century, in *The Canterbury Tales*. It's an unfinished epic that traces a pilgrimage from London to Canterbury. Along the way many of the pilgrims tell their stories in monologue to while away the tedium of the trip."

"I take it that's also one of those interactive monologue things," Fred says.

"Yes."

"Well, do you have a short series of monologues we can use to illustrate?"

"Sure. It's not interactive, but each monologue tells the speaker's story, just as Browning and Pound did. It's called . . . ,"

Bordello

Hank Fedder

Hank Fedder is my name. My wife is Maud
Fedder—she's a good woman, the neighbors
say. And she is, I guess. She's sure no bawd,
and that's God's truth. Goodness just about pours
out of her. Depends on what you call "good,"
of course. She's good in the house, out of doors,
at market, in her clubs—just anyplace.
Except in bed. There, she rubs my face

in the "dirt" she calls my "male mind." She makes
me sick of myself, of what I need to
do. She cuts my guts out, and then she takes
what's left of me, sets it in the window
like a dummy, calls it "Hubby," "Dad," bakes
cakes for it, and sends it off to work. Oh,
yes, she's good all right. She makes a fine spouse.
On her bridge night I come to this whorehouse

to salvage what's left of my need, of my
insides. It never works. I leave here done
to death with sickness, the sickness that I
have now, truly, just as she claims. She's won
her point. I'm not the man she married by
a long shot—no man at all. And my son,
our son . . . he knows it, hates the "hubby" of
that best of mothers he will always love.

Jasper Olson

I take my women any way they come—
I'm Jasper Olson, brother. Hard and fast
I play this game. Though some folks think I'm dumb,
I take my women any way they come,

and come they do. There's no time to be numb
in this life—grab it now and ram the past.
I take my women any way they come.
I'm Jasper Olson, brother, hard and fast.

Jonathan Hawkins

For as many nights as there are
days in the month, I come here to
sleep with a woman. The first star
sees me climb the hill, for my cue
is a point of light—oddly, you
may think. But the light floats upon
a vast shadow. My name is Jon
Hawkins . . . Jonathan, but none call
me that. I come here and knock on
this door that opens. And that's all,

or almost. It is not far
to climb the hill from the town. Few
people see me, not that I care
anyway. I'm past all that. Two
or three townsfolk might stick their blue
noses in the air still. I'm stone
to them. The old Hawkins mansion
was sold years back. Few would recall
my father, or my father's son.
This door that opens (and that's all)

opens for a wastrel. A jar
full of fireflies, an untrue
flame—that's this house to me: the instar
that never became a moth, who
was born but not transformed. I grew,
yes, but not enough. What makes one
man want to try to reach the sun;
another, want a candle? Tall
he was, my father. He would shun
this door that opens. And that's all

my story. Still . . . I am not done.
I come here to win what is won
easily, and I cannot fall
far. I touch, out of my dungeon,
this door that opens, and that's all.

Will Somers

The sun shone all day
like a bright cock preening
for its hen. Making hay
lay over the greening
grass. There is no meaning
hidden for you to trace
in these wishes leaning
like moonlight on my face,

for I live as I may—
I, Will Somers—gleaning
in all weathers. I say,
"lay over the greening
world well, the wind keening
or soughing." Woman's grace
is but a night's dreaming,
like moonlight on my face:

a thing met with on the way,
taken without scheming.
I never married. Clay
lay over the greening
sap of my youth. Steaming
nights I spent alone; lace
fancies all went streaming
like moonlight on my face,

like sweat. Sweat, careening,
lay over the greening
fields. Now, I know love's place,
like moonlight on my face.

Simon Judson

In this dark place I am still with God.
Here I read the pages of man's lust,
seek the revelation of the sod,
remind the flesh again, "Thou art dust."

I am not of this town. Reverend
Mister Simon Judson is my name,
and my parish is down at the end
of Route 40, miles away. I came
here first just about a year ago—
accidentally, of course. I must
be honest; I would not go a rod
for sensual satisfaction. No,
I come to this house because I must
seek the revelation of the sod,

not because my life is cold. I lend
my soul to my flock weekly. The same
is true *in re* my family. To mend
my spirit, I renew it in shame
at the fount of blood, as the saints do.
I drive long distances, for great blame
would attend me were I found out. Trust
and good faith are my stock in trade, so
I spare no pains to avoid a nod,
remind the flesh again, "Thou art dust,"

and keep peace. Even my closest friend
might not understand my pilgrim aim.
This sinful hovel is a Godsend,
truly. Here all the worst vices flame
out of the Pit for my study—glow
and glitter like Sodom. That I know
man's follies first-hand is fact—disgust
and degradation; the mire, the rust
of will—here I am armored and shod!
Here I read the pages of man's lust. . . .
In this dark place I am still with God.

Rick de Travaille

Having fallen down the manhole,
I discovered myself to be
in the wrong world. Having no soul
was a problem at first for me,
but I, Rick de Travaille, ignore
the problem now. I split this door
where the women are, and I find
in the flesh a little peace of mind.

Jason Potter

Suddenly, nothing was left of all those
years we'd spent together in the same house,
under that old mansard that bent and rose
above us, gracefully guarding. The spruce

in the dooryard spired out of the grass
like a steeple, pulling us taut as bows—
both generations. But age is a noose:
suddenly, nothing was left of all those

mornings and nights. I, Jason Potter, chose
to lay away my helpmeet and my spouse
in a lone bed. So ended my repose.
Years we'd spent together in the same house

became beads to tell, the string broken—loose
time come unstrung. Still, outside, the spruce grows,
and it is nature to try to mend loss.
Under that old mansard that bent and rose

over the life we'd built, my blood still flows
in fever now and then. I make my truce
with flesh through these paid women whom I use.
Above us, guarding and graceful, the spruce

used to seem a symbol of common use
and fulfillment of self and heart—those blues
tipping sheer limbs sharply; strong and close
and clean, the bole and needles of pure hues. . . .
Suddenly, nothing was left.

Lafe Grat

In this house I am not ugly—nowhere
else. Nor is there
a mirror in the room we use, my bought
bride and I. What
images are reflected in her eyes
I recognize
as in a dream only, my face redrawn
by night. Reborn
each evening of this woman, spared my name,
the cruel fame
of the publicly disfigured, I roar
with my old whore
like a whole man, transfigured for a time.
Sordid? I am
Lafe Grat. I work hard to make a living.
There's no giving
to a man who makes you think of darkness,
for my likeness
is found buried in everyone, hidden
till, unbidden,
it rises to gorge the beast in the blood.
So, out of mud
I am formed and rise each morning to stalk
where others walk
in a world of surfaces—till night when,
like other men,
I may purchase with coin my manhood, life—
a moment's wife.

Tom Biggins

The sun is blue and the sky is yellow gold;
Yes, sun is blue, sky is a yellow gold.
I once was young, but now I'm growing old.

The grass is brown, the loam is turning green.
We have brown grass, loam has turned to green.
I'm sixty now. I wish I was sixteen.

If I were young again the sun would shine
Copper bright in a sky of purple wine,
And I would think the women all were fine—

As fine as silk, welcoming as the lake
I used to swim in for my body's sake—
And each of them would be for me to take.

But I am old now. Nothing I can do
Beneath this yellow sky, for the sun is blue.

ENVOY:

The Wind Carol

The townspeople peer out of their windows—
the black snow falls, and the wind blows.

From each imprisoning flake that falls
an image looks out at the walls
of faces, and a thin voice calls
to the townspeople peering out of their windows.

Melisande comes drifting down
out of the air above the town,
recalling the lace of her wedding gown,
the years like snow in the wind that blows.

The Captain falls, epaulettes gleaming,
through a pine where the wind's streaming
rustles, then rises like missiles screaming
toward the enemy's thin windows.

These are cold voices that comprise
this dark wind touching a storm of eyes—

Mary, trapped in her bit of hoar,
gazes out of her dim mirror
thinking of lovers outside her door
lashing, like limbs, in the wind that blows.

Old Tom remembers some fleeting kiss
which he'd thought lost, but was caught like this
within his mind's paralysis
of moments frozen behind windows.

And as it falls or drifts, each face,
stunned in an attitude of grace
or of despair, looks for its place
among its kind in the wind that blows.

These are cold voices that comprise
this dark wind touching a storm of eyes.
The townspeople peer out of their windows;
the black snow falls, and the wind blows.

Chapter 2

Speech in Narration

"Those were interesting!" Fred says. "You're right, each monologue was a whole story. Except for that last one."

"Yes, the speakers stop speaking and the Author steps back to
look at the whole picture."

"He sort of sums up the human condition, you might say,"
Fred says.

"You might."

"And the poems rhyme, too."

"Not merely rhyme, they have meters as well."

"Meters?"

"Yes, more or less regular rhythms. In fact, the poems are all
written in strict verse forms, most of them traditional."

"What would be the difference between a traditional verse
form and one that's not?"

"Nonce."

"What?" Fred is clearly baffled.

"Not 'not,' *nonce*. Many poets make up their own forms on the
spot rather than falling back on such things as sonnets, sestinas,
ballades, and so forth. Such made-up forms are called *nonce forms*."

"That makes nonce sense," Fred says. He grins rather widely.
"Where would I find out about such things?"

"In one of this book's companion volumes," the Author replies, "*The Book of Forms, A Handbook of Poetics.*

Tag Lines

"But we're going to go on now. Did you notice not only in the poems but in the prose fiction piece, 'Savants,' that we didn't have to use quotation marks or tag lines either?"

Fred looks worried. He clears his throat and squints at the screen.

"Something wrong, Fred?"

"Okay," he says, blushing, "what's a tag line?"

"A tag line is a couple of words or a phrase that tells you who is speaking. The simplest and least obtrusive tag lines are 'he said' and 'she said,' or minor variations, like 'she replied' or 'he asked,' as in this conversation between a man named Horace and a woman named Gail":

"Hello," he said, "my name's Harold Wilkinson. What's yours?" he asked.

"Hi," she replied, turning in her chair to look at him. "I'm Gail Adams."

"Pleased to meet you," Harold said. "I've been watching you for about an hour."

Fred looks thoughtful. "That's kind of blah, it seems to me. Can't you jazz that up a bit?"

"Sure," the Author replies, "but it's best to keep things simple. Using adjectives, adverbs, and fancy verbs to describe tone of voice or show what's going on just gets in the way of the action and characterization. This is what can happen":

"Hello," he croaked nervously, "my name's Harold Wilkinson. What's yours?" he asked with as much aplomb as he could muster.

"Hi," she squeaked uncertainly, turning in her chair to look at him. "I'm Gail Adams," she said blushingly.

"Pleased to meet you," Harold declared. "I've been watching you for about an hour," he offered with a quaver in his voice.

Fred nods. "I see what you mean. The dialogue looks sort of amateurish, too—stilted and forced. What's the reason for that?"

"It's called 'author intrusion.' The wish of a modern author generally is to create the illusion of reality, to make the reader forget he or she is reading a story rather than living it. Therefore, an author tries to hide himself or herself, to make the story *seem* as natural as possible. Adjectives and other sorts of descriptions tend to remind the reader that somebody's controlling his or her interest."

"But can't that scene be jazzed up another way," Fred asks, "and still keep the action and characterization going?"

In Medias Res

"Sure. You can even start *in medias res*."

"What in blazes does *that* mean? Fred is scowling again. "Talk about fancy words!"

"Well, once in a while you have to use writers' jargon," the Author says. Clearly annoyed, he glares at Fred. "It's Latin for 'in the middle of things,' and that's where you're supposed to start a narrative, so as to get the action going and the reader involved. In fact, here's that same scene as it was originally written as the beginning of a short story titled 'An Old-Fashioned Kind of Guy'":

"Gail Adams," she replied. "And yours?"

"Harold Wilkinson. I've been watching you for about an hour, and I finally couldn't help approaching you. Forgive me." He sat down and put his cup of coffee on the table. She was beautiful.

She shrugged. "What's to forgive? And if you're going to ask me for a date, I accept." She made her mouth stop brooding for a second, but her eyes stayed dark. She must have seen surprise or discomfort in his, because she said, "I'm on the rebound, as they say, and I'm looking for dates."

"That really *does* get things going!" A look of admiration has replaced boredom in Fred's eyes. "And Harold never even asks his question—it's been asked before the story begins. Not bad! Not bad at all! You're even beginning to characterize them. The only description I see in the first three lines," he pauses to look over the story opening again, "is the predicate adjective 'beautiful' in 'She was beautiful.' So 'keep it simple' is the watchword, right? At least so far as tag lines go."

"Right. Adjectives and adverbs are the mark of the amateur. Let the characters do their thing and the narrative moves right along. Don't slow it down. Here's the whole story."

An Old-Fashioned Kind of Guy

"Gail Adams," she replied. "And yours?"

"Harold Wilkinson. I've been watching you for about an hour, and I finally couldn't help approaching you. Forgive me." He sat down and put his cup of coffee on the table. She was beautiful.

She shrugged. "What's to forgive? And if you're going to ask me for a date, I accept." She made her mouth stop brooding for a second, but her eyes stayed dark. She must have seen surprise or discomfort in his, because she said, "I'm on the rebound, as they say, and I'm looking for dates."

The sounds of the college snack bar began buzzing in Harold's ears. He looked around, but none of the other young people were paying any attention to them. He felt relieved—things weren't going as he had been planning for the last half hour or so. That is, they were and they weren't.

"What's the matter?" she asked and stared at him.

"The hell with it," Harold said. "I'll take it that way if that's the way it has to be. Pride be damned." She really smiled then. She reached out and touched him on the wrist, grinned, and shook her long dark hair around her shoulders.

They walked across campus together, mostly in silence. Spring was beginning to make its big play of the year—just barely beginning. He was surprised when she asked, again, "What's the matter?" Harold thought of giving a clever answer then decided against it.

"It's you," he said, "you've put me off my stride and I don't like it." He shook his head. "But I like you well enough to try to get my balance back. Every time I try you trip me again." He stopped and struck a heroic pose. "I wish to be master of my own fate!"

"Like, when did I trip you?" Gail asked, laughing. The fake carillon—records and loudspeakers—began playing atop the administration building as she reached out and took his hand.

"Like just now." Harold sighed deeply and squeezed her fingers just a bit. He could feel in his belly the familiar excitement of infatuation in its early stages, but then, as her light grip responded to his, something clamped down on whatever it was that was rising in him and he felt chilly. He shivered and, with his free hand, snapped a bud off a hedge they were passing.

"It'll be all right," Gail said. "You'll see." He raised one eyebrow and looked at her a moment. She laughed again, lightly. Harold liked the music of it. "Here's my dorm."

They stopped in front of the glass doors with the decals of the college crest on them. The afternoon sun glinted on the glass and threw an aura around her hair, turning it warm as she stood facing him, her back to the entranceway. Harold unfocused his eyes so that he could look through her and beyond. He saw that now she had not only an aura, but a halo as well—the round college seal circled her head exactly. The word EXCEL-SIOR was a tiara perched upon the back of her head.

"My lady," he said, "you are a very queen of spring. A sylph of bright air, nymph of the forest, whose spirit invests the afternoon with light brighter than that of the paling sun!" He tugged at his forelock and bowed. He more than halfway meant it.

He thought she would laugh again, but her lips had a downward bend as she said, "Watch your language."

Harold thought about what he had just said but couldn't figure what it was she objected to. He decided it was just the general corniness of the whole speech. "Square," Harold said aloud, but to himself. "Not you!" He made a gesture, and her expression softened once more—"Something I was thinking about myself."

"It's okay. I just don't like that word."

"What word?" Harold asked, still puzzled.

"Nymph." Gail said. "See you tonight, then?" She turned and pushed the doors open. "About seven-thirty?"

"Right. Excelsior!" Harold said again, but this time rather abstract-edly. He waved, feeling again the heat and chill in his belly. The campus was nearly empty as he hurried over the spongy grass to the dining hall.

The only program on campus that evening was a concert at the Little Theatre, and Harold took Gail there. A famous chamber music group was performing, and by the time they got there the hall was pretty well full. Harold showed his student I.D. and Gail showed hers. They managed to find two seats together. The weather had turned chilly again, but the theater was too warm, so everyone was shucking as much outer clothing as possible. Harold helped Gail with her jacket and they finally got settled. Gail looked through the program. Her finger stopped at a title. "What's this?" she asked.

Harold leaned over to look and noticed the perfume she was wearing—it curled about him and he breathed deeply.

"That's nice," he said.

"What?"

"I said, that's a concerto for harpsichord and jazz ensemble. Smells wild."

She looked at him. "What?"

"Sounds wild." He grimaced at her.

"You're a screwball," and she turned away in a mock huff.

Harold let his hand fall gently on her arm. It was soft, like her perfume. Suddenly he felt her muscles stiffen under the cashmere. He glanced up, startled, and followed the line of her gaze. He saw nothing but some art faculty and their wives sitting nearby. Harold looked around, but nothing unusual was going on.

"Harold," Gail said in a hard whisper, "I'm sorry. I don't feel well. Let's leave. Please."

"But we just got here!"

"Please," she said again. She began to get up.

Harold rose too, grabbed her coat, and they made their way to the vestibule where he helped her on with her things. She barely stopped walking. In only a few seconds they were back outside. Harold had to step fast to keep up with her.

"What's going on?" Harold had begun to feel some anger.

"Don't ask any questions," Gail replied. "Let's just go. Where's your car?"

Harold pointed and they headed toward the parking lot. "Go where?" He took her arm and as he did so he could feel the breeze come up in a gust. It still had a lot of winter in it.

"I don't know." There was a catch in her voice. "Do you live in a dorm?"

"Yes. Farley. Why?"

"Would your roommate be likely to be in?"

"He's studying for a test tomorrow."

"Then let's try a motel," she said. "Do you have enough money?"

There was a knot in his belly suddenly, a hot snag. "I own some plastic money." He could think of nothing else to say. He tightened his grip on her arm and they walked in a pulsing stillness to the car. They got in. Harold pulled out of the row of cars onto the service road and shortly they were driving at a good clip down Route Twelve.

"Slow it down," Gail told him. "We don't want to get picked up."

Harold pulled his aching foot up off the accelerator and the car slipped down to the speed limit. He could still think of nothing to say, nothing he wanted to say, so he kept his eyes on the road till a motel appeared over the hill. He pulled in. "Be right back," he said.

Their room was at the end of the row of doors in the low, flat facade of the single building. There were few cars in the lot. He moved the car, parked, and they got out—Gail didn't wait for Harold to help her. She walked to the door of the room and waited until he came around from the far side. She looked small as she huddled with crossed arms in her fur-collared coat under the door light.

Harold fumbled with the key, opened the door, and they went in. The room was small, too full of cheap furniture and a television set. A big mirror hung on the wall over a low chest of drawers at the foot of one of the twin double beds. Gail, still huddled in her coat, went over and sat down on the bed with the mirror.

Harold closed the door, locked it, and stood looking at her. For a few moments the silence continued and they could hear faint sounds from another room—it sounded like a sitcom. At last Gail looked up, straight at him.

"Well," she said, "what are we waiting for?" She stood, took off her coat, and threw it on the other bed. Harold followed suit and went to her.

"I've never even kissed you," he said. Gail closed her eyes and Harold stroked her cheek, smelled the perfume again. He kissed her, not as roughly as he thought he wanted to. At first she was slack in his arms and her lips were too pliant, but she began to respond. Harold could feel the pressure of her body all along his.

Gail pushed him away, not hard, took off her clothes, and lay down on the bed. Her eyes were so dark that Harold felt as though he were falling into them. The room spun lazily around him and a pipe creaked. He willed the furniture to sit still, and things settled down, but even so, now and then a chair seemed to make a vague start at motion in the corners of his vision. He stood looking down at this girl he had met only that afternoon. The moments were lengthening themselves. "Like what you see?" she asked.

Even as he felt the turmoil in his stomach a vise was closing off feeling. Harold began to panic. He had come this far. . . . "Hell," he said, and stripped. He knelt on the bed beside her. His fingers ran over her long, cool thighs, and she trembled. He glanced up and saw them framed in the mirror.

A small sound—a moan or a sigh—escaped her as he touched her breasts. She closed her eyes. "Come on," she said.

It was difficult for Harold to breathe. He got into position over her and felt her pressing up against him. It might have been all right if she hadn't opened her eyes just then. If he hadn't seen what he thought he saw. It was as though he'd swallowed a gallon of ice water. "This is a hell of a way to get even with him," Harold said. The fires were all the way out. "He'll never know, and you'll just have to keep doing this."

"Christ, what are you talking about?" She spat the words.

"Come on, damn you!" She reached up and pulled him down, but it was too late. Harold rolled over and lay on his back beside her.

"You said you were on the rebound," Harold said. "It was one of those art professors at the concert, wasn't it?" The ceiling stretched to its edges. Everything was solid. "Tell you what, Gail. I'll marry you instead." Harold said it flatly. It should have been a surprise for him to realize he meant it, but it wasn't.

"You'll . . . marry . . . me." She said it in the dull voice of an android. "You rat," she said. "You fucking—no, you non-fucking rat!" She sat up and looked at him. "What makes you think you're so much better than everybody else?" Harold flinched when she moved her arm as though to hit him, but she didn't follow through.

"Me?" he said, "I? My lady, I am no superior being but only a mere and temporary mortal to whom it has been given to suffer. I have proffered my hand in good faith, as being the logical thing to do under the circumstances. Those circumstances being I'm mad about you and your body, even upon such abrupt and tentative relationship as we have established." He rolled his eyes and so did she, but she meant it.

"Oh, lord," she said, "you do think you're God. You think you can come along, pick me up, and turn me into plaster-of-Paris." She flopped down on the bed, reached for her purse, and got out a cigarette. She lit it and lay back on the pillow inhaling the smoke deeply, letting it out in a long, cloudy breath. "If you're so hot for my body, why didn't you take it when you had the chance?"

Harold lay thinking about that for a while. "Because," he said at last, "I don't want it this way. I don't want you to use me to get even with somebody. I told you, you keep putting me off balance, and I don't like to be off balance. I turned you down to get my equilibrium back and to help you find yours again. Then we can start over, like lovers." He talked slowly, figuring things out as he went along.

Gail snorted. "You see what I mean? You're so hung up on being rational it even affects your glands. You figure you're going to fix the world, don't you? That's a laugh." She got up on one elbow and looked down sideways at him. Her breast floated like a lush moon before him.

"You're on the rebound. When you stop bouncing we'll talk about it."

"Like hell we will. Rebound!" She stared at him. "You'll believe anything, won't you? She gritted her teeth and bent down toward him. Harold stared at her but it was difficult, she was so close. She kissed him, very tenderly, and he closed his eyes to enjoy it. He felt himself sinking again.

"One more time," she said. "Take it." Her hand moved over his belly, stroking, traveling downward. Once again he felt the fire and the ice, that vise of chill closing off what he wanted to feel.

"No," he said. "Not this way."

She was off the bed and getting into her clothes in a second. Harold watched her momentarily, then got up and dressed himself. They said nothing. He turned off the lights as they left. "One more time," he said as they stood in the dark outdoors. "Marry me."

"Shit," she said, and got into the car.

Pace

"Another thing I notice," Fred says, still looking at the monitor, "is how fast the scenes move. But you don't always want scenes to move that fast, do you?"

The Author sits back and stretches. He glances out the big attic window in the wall to his left, beyond his desk, the window that looks down on West Eighth Street. The medium-sized maple tree right outside obscures his view of the opposite side of the road—it's in full leaf. He forces his attention back to the matter in hand. "Certainly not. Some scenes require a fast pace. So fast sometimes, in fact, that you don't want tag lines to appear at all, and you don't want to slow the dialogue down even with other kinds of writing, such as mood-setting or authorial characterization."

"Who writes like that?"

Dialect 1

"Well, John O'Hara did it in several of his novels including *Appointment in Samara*. Here's a passage in which Julian is speaking with Caroline—and let's make a note to talk about this again when we get to a point where we can discuss dialect":

He started the car again. "Hyuh, baby," he said. "What were we talking about? Had we finished with Chuck?"

"Mm."

"What's the mattah, honey sugah lamb pie, what's the mattah you all?"

"Listen, Ju. Listen to me, will you?"

"Listen to you? Why, Mrs. English, one of the most attractive features of the Cadillac is the minimum of noise in the motor. Just let me show—"

"No. don't be funny."

"What's the matter? Did I do something wrong? Did I say something? Christ, I thought we were getting along fine."

"We were, but something you said worried me. See you don't even remember saying it."

"What did I say?"

"When you stopped the car. When you got out to fix the chain, you said something about you were going to fix it now, while you were sober."

"Oh," he said.

"As if—"

"I get it. You don't have to draw a map."

"How's that for fast-paced?"

"Okay," Fred says, "but how about a little contrast now. How can you slow it down?"

"We can try a little Christopher Isherwood, who was both a playwright and a novelist. Here's how he wanted a rather slow scene in his novel *The Memorial*":

"What do you think of it?"

"I think it's absolutely marvelous," she'd say, beaming super-gratitude at him, as though he'd written book music and was taking all the parts.

"Not too bad, is it?" She could hear his joy, his pride in the revue ring like a telephone bell through his drawl.

And then she'd ask him about the office and whether the work was very hard and how he liked it. And he began to tell her, carefully and seriously, suddenly breaking off with:

"You're absolutely certain I'm not boring you?"

"You'll notice," the Author says, "that Isherwood here is giving the reader the impression of a slow-moving, even a boring conversation, but he doesn't want to bore us readers to death in the process. Do you see what he does to get around the problem?"

Format and Punctuation 1

Fred grins. "Sure, he just *describes* the conversation, in part at least, when he writes, 'And he began to tell her, carefully and seriously, suddenly breaking off with:

"""You're absolutely certain I'm not boring you?"""

"That's great punctuation, Fred. Within your own quote (" ") you quote some other material, which goes into single quotes (' '), and that material also has a quotation in it, so you go to double quotes again (""" """). You're learning fast! Pretty soon you'll want to be an author yourself, if I don't watch out!" The Author grins broadly.

Nonconversations 1: Summary Dialogue

Fred squints. There is an odd gleam in his eye.

"But let's make sure we don't carry this *description of a conversation* business too far. Usually if we find that sort of thing in a story, especially by a novice writer, it means the writer is uncomfortable with dialogue and is trying to avoid writing it. Isherwood used nonconversation for a special purpose, to slow the pace, and he used it well."

"Are there other ways to slow the pace of dialogue in the dialogue itself?"

Narration 2: Frame Narration

"There's *frame narration*."

"What's that?"

"This begins to get us back to the question of narration that we raised when we began 'Savants.' Every story has a narrator, but narration isn't usually considered to be dialogue, though it's clearly somebody talking. In the case of 'Savants' it was a major character who was narrating, but the narration in that story was clearly a monologue, which is a form of dialogue.

"Frame narration also muddies the waters between narration and dialogue," the Author continues, "and the grand master of frame narration is Joseph Conrad. Let's take a look at his novel *Heart of Darkness;* here's how it begins (I'm not going to use quotation marks except for actual speeches by people, so bear that in mind, okay?)":

The Nellie, a cruising yawl, swung to her anchor without a flutter of the sails, and was at rest.

"Who's that talking, Fred?"

"That's obviously the author narrating the story."

"But it's not. Two paragraphs later Conrad sets the characters, and we discover that the narrator is a character in the story, one of four people, but *not* the one named Marlow."

"How do we know those things?"

"The next sentence I'll quote tells you":

The Director of Companies was our captain and our host. We four affectionately watched his back as he stood in the bows looking to seaward.

"Who were the four?" Fred asks.

The lawyer—the best of old fellows—had, because of his many years and many virtues, the only cushion on deck, and was lying on the only rug. The Accountant had brought out already a box of dominoes, and was toying architecturally with the bones. Marlow sat cross-legged right aft, leaning against the mizzen-mast. He had sunken cheeks, a yellow complexion, a straight back, an ascetic aspect, and, with his arms dropped, the palms of hands outwards, resembled an idol.

"So the author's not narrating," Fred observes, "and neither is Marlow."

"But Marlow is going to be a major player—in fact, he is the real protagonist of the novel, although a fellow named Mr. Kurtz at first appears to be.

"After some scene-setting and mood inducement, here's what happens":

"And this also," said Marlow suddenly, "has been one of the dark places of the earth."

"That begins the narration of Marlow's adventure. There's a little more mood inducement, but after that Marlow tells the story—*he* is the 'frame narrator' of the novel. Clearly, this sort of narrative is a monologue, and every once in a while Conrad has to remind the reader that it's still really a minor character who is telling the *overall* story, which includes the story the frame narrator is telling."

"How does he do that?" Fred asks, leaning forward and brushing the hair out of his glinty eyes.

"Well, after a very long piece of frame narration—pages of it, in fact, Conrad does this":

... *"It seems to me I am trying to tell you a dream—making a vain attempt, because no relation of a dream can convey the dream-sensation, that commingling of absurdity, surprise, and bewilderment in a tremor of struggling revolt, that notion of being captured by the incredible which is of the very essence of dreams ... "*

He was silent for a while.

" ... No, it is impossible; it is impossible to convey the life-sensation of any given epoch of one's existence—that which makes its truth, its meaning—its subtle and penetrating essence. It is impossible. We live, as we dream—alone ... "

He paused again as if reflecting, then added—

"Of course in this you fellows see more than I could then. You see me, whom you know ... "

It had become so pitch dark that we listeners could hardly see one another.

"So that's frame narration," Fred says.

"That's it."

"Can we go back to 'Savants' for a bit?"

The Author nods. "Why not?"

Fred hesitates for a moment. "In that story it was the main character, the protagonist, who was delivering a monologue."

Diction 2: Characterization

"Right, just as in *Heart of Darkness,* except that she was the narrator, not the frame narrator. Every story must have a narrator and a protagonist as a basic minimum. Sometimes they're the same person, but often they're not. What was she like? You heard her, but did you see her as well? As a person, I mean."

Fred nods vigorously, his thin hair falling down across his fore-head. He raises his left hand and brushes it back. "Sure. She was a housewife who lived in an ordinary neighborhood. She had very little education—you could tell that by the way she spoke."

"That's diction again—I mentioned it earlier. Her level of diction was not very high. Her vocabulary was limited—she used no big words, and she mispronounced the biggest word in the story—the French word *savant* which means 'wise person.' She had no frame of reference for it, so she equated it with the English word that sounded most like it—*servant*."

"Even that confusion helped to characterize her," Fred says, leaning forward. "After all, she was a servant to this kid she had who was severely retarded. She was stuck with this child that she both loved and hated, with a husband who wanted to get rid of their child and who didn't like his wife much. She was desperate."

"Desperate and hopeless. And finally she broke."

"She had so many conflicts," Fred says, "but the main one was internal."

"Was there any action in the story?"

Fred thinks about that for a minute. "Not any direct action that the reader could see, though the narrator/protagonist tells us about a scene that was filled with action, when she took out all her frustrations on her child and abused him physically."

"Action is the best way to characterize someone, but speech is the second-best way—the speech of the person being character-ized, and then the speech of other characters talking about that person. Here's an example of that from Robert B. Parker's 2002 book titled *Widow's Walk;* it's a dialogue between Parker's detec-tive character Spenser and his psychologist girlfriend, Susan":

"You're working for that hussy again," Susan said.
"Rita?"
"Miss Predatory," Susan said.
"I like Rita," I said.
"I know."

"Are you being jealous?"

"Analytic," Susan said. *"Rita is sexually rapacious and perfectly amoral about it. I'm merely acknowledging that."*

"But you don't disapprove."

"Professionalism prevents disapproval," Susan said.

"So the term 'hussy' is just a clinical designation," I said.

"Certainly," Susan said. *"She has every right to wear her skirts as short as she wishes."*

"She wears short skirts?" I said.

"Like you didn't notice."

"So do you like Rita, Ms. Professional?"

"Red-haired floozy," Susan said.

"I so admire professionalism."

"That's great!" Fred says. "All three people are characterized, and you don't even meet Rita."

"Parker is a master of dialogue in fiction, but let's get back to 'Savants.' Was the story dramatic?"

"Almost *too* dramatic. Maybe, in fact, melodramatic."

"I hope not," the Author replies, "but in any case, the first thing one has to learn about fiction is that conflict and problem are at the root of any dramatic situation and, generally speaking, a dramatic situation is the basis for all storytelling."

"No wonder fiction and drama have so much in common. Is it possible that some stories are actually plays?"

"'Savants' is actually a play. If it were read aloud it would be no different from any other monologue seen on stage. In fact, to turn it into a stage production all you'd have to do for a scene is put the monologist into a kitchen with another woman."

"Are there any *famous* stories like that?" Fred asks.

Anyone watching might be able to see the hair bristle on the Author's neck. But he is a professional, and he controls himself after a moment's pause.

"Well, there's a story by Jamaica Kincaid titled 'Girl' that's appearing in a lot of anthologies these days. It appears at first to be a monologue, but in fact it's a dialogue because a second person speaks two sentences. There's no scene-setting, but we soon understand that a mother is teaching her daughter, whom she doesn't trust, to be a West Indian homemaker. The whole story is in fact made up of one huge sentence and is barely more than a page long. The mother lays down rule after rule. The daughter tries, twice, to interrupt, once with a protest of innocence, once with a question. It's no use: the acid-tongued mother rolls right on. The daughter's dialogue is given in italics, right in the middle of the mother's speech."

Empathy

"I can see that's close to being a play," Fred says. "Mainly just one person talking—the mother's voice, with no descriptions or 'she said.' But the daughter sounds like such an underdog. I think I'd probably like her better, even though she has only two lines. Better than the mother, who has most of the speech."

"It's human conflict in which we are interested, and that holds true even if our main character is an animal, or a bird, or an insect, or whatever, for the creature at the heart of the story will display human characteristics with which we can empathize."

"What's the difference between empathy and sympathy?"

Fred is having trouble with his limp pompadour, first because it's so hot and muggy in the attic room—it's July, and the Author works in a garret—and, second, because he is fanning himself with some of the pages of the manuscript.

"Hey! Put those down!"

Fred gets up suddenly and goes to the big window that looks down on West Eighth Street. He knows if he could stick his head out the window and look left, he'd probably be able to see Lake Ontario at the bottom of the hill.

"Stop doing exposition," he says to the Author testily, "and answer my question. But first, how about if I turn on the air conditioner?" At the bottom of the window an air conditioner is built into the wall. The canopy window itself is open—it's a bit like a glass awning that winds outward at the bottom.

"Okay, but close the window first," the Author says. "It *is* getting hot. Just turn that knob on the left and set it on high. That's it." The rush of cool air begins to hum into the room. Fred wipes his brow and brushes back his forelock.

"Empathy is a feeling *with,*" the Author taps out on his keyboard. "We put ourselves in the place of the creature or the person struggling. Empathy is stronger than sympathy which is a feeling *for* something or someone, from the outside. Remember back under *Viewpoint 1* when I mentioned subjective and objective access? Well, think of it this way: empathy is subjective, getting inside another person's character and situation. When we experience empathy, we are identifying with another being, becoming one with it, in effect. Sympathy is more objective, though it's still fellow-feeling."

"Sort of, 'There, but for the grace of God, go I,' as opposed to, 'This is happening to me as it happens to my fellow.'" Fred purses his lips and knits his brows. "A while back you said that a story has to have at least a narrator and a protagonist. . . ."

"And that they are sometimes one and the same. That's right. What's the matter?"

Fred is shaking his head vigorously, as though he is trying to loosen up cobwebs that are clouding his sight. "My head's starting to spin. I've got so many questions I hardly know what to ask first."

"Calm down, Fred." The Author rises and pats Fred on the shoulder.

Characterization by Nomenclature

"Hey!" Fred yells. The Author jumps back, startled. "How come I don't have a last name?"

"What do you need a last name for? The women in 'Savants' had no names at all."

Fred just gives the author a cold, sardonic stare.

"Okay, we'll go with characterization by nomenclature—your last name is Foyle . . . Fred Foyle. How's that?"

Fred groans. "I had to ask."

"Well, that's your name. Judging from the spelling you're probably an Irish-American. Now, what's your question?"

Subject and Theme

"This may seem as though it's coming out of left field, but, okay—what's the difference between subject and theme?"

"That's easy. A subject is what you're talking about, and it can be expressed in a word or a phrase: *Love* is a subject. But a theme is what you say about a subject, and it can be expressed *only* in a complete sentence: 'Love is a many-splintered thing' is a theme. Note that the subject of our story is also the subject of our sentence."

"What's the situation? Lovers making out on a wooden bench?" Fred snickers.

"You think you're being funny, Fred, but in fact if you write a story illustrating that theme, you have to choose your elements so as to back it. *All* the other aspects of the story, including the situation, must support the theme."

"Does dialogue have any particular part in subject and theme?" Fred leans forward a little to get a bit further into the flow of air from the conditioner. It blows his thin hair about a bit.

"Sure. Take 'Girl' for instance. Since the whole story is a dialogue, the only way the author can express the theme is through the speech of one of the characters. The theme of the story is in the last line, spoken by the antagonist, the mother. To paraphrase, she says to her daughter, 'You mean you're not going to turn out to be a slut after all? Maybe I've misjudged you.' Here's a story that's nothing but theme. In order to make this work, we have to do damage to motivation."

"What's that all about?"

"Well, a persona must act in character, and his or her reasons for acting at all must be good ones—that's motivation. We've all heard people say, 'If you do such and such, I'll kill you.' But do we really think someone's going to be killed for a peccadillo?"

"A *what?*" Fred asks.

"Something minor, like getting a dress dirty."

One Sunday Morning

Mary Elizabeth's breaking one of the best teacups was nearly the last straw. After she had cleaned up the mess, Mrs. Taylor hustled her daughter upstairs to get her ready for Sunday school.

"Now look, Mary Elizabeth," Mrs. Taylor said, "you're all nice and clean, and I want you to stay that way." Helen Taylor caught a glimpse of herself in the mirror over Mary Elizabeth's chest of drawers and pursed her lips ruefully. When she was tired like this it always looked as though she were older than she ought to be. She was in her middle twenties, but sometimes she looked thirty or over, as for instance now, after a morning of struggling with her hyperactive five-year-old. Helen Taylor felt a stirring of frustrated and resentful anger, but she put it down. She did not believe in anger. Helen ran a hand through her hair and looked back at Mary Elizabeth.

While she was buttoning up the little girl's dress John called up the stairs. "I'm running down to the drug store for the paper, hon," he said. "Be right back." Before Helen could reply she heard the door slam, and a second or two later the car door opened and closed, the motor revved up, and he was gone down the Sunday street. Helen sighed and listened for a moment to a bird singing outside the window in the summer sunlight.

"Mommy, can I go outside?" Mary Elizabeth looked up at her mother pleadingly.

Helen had been planning to have John watch Mary while she got herself ready for church, and she hesitated for a second. "Okay, Mary Elizabeth, but you're all dressed up clean for Sunday school, so you stay right in the front yard. And don't get your pretty yellow dress dirty or mommy will murder you. Right?"

"Right," Mary Elizabeth said, and grinned. Helen listened to Mary's footsteps running down the stairs, heard the front door open and close, and then she went into her own room to get ready.

John came back after having been gone for half an hour or so. He had run into a friend at the drugstore, and they had chatted over a cup of coffee. When he opened the front door of his house, the paper under his arm, he found Mary Elizabeth hanging in the hallway, a piece of clothesline knotted around her neck and a big mud stain on her bodice. He tried to scream, but the sound was strangled and came out a croak.

Helen was sitting in the rocking chair just inside the door into the living room. Her eyes were calm as they met John's. "Well, I told her what would happen if she got dirty," Helen said. "Don't blame me."

When the police came, elbowing their way through the crowd of muttering and whispering neighbors, Helen was still sitting in the chair and John was sobbing and coughing, exhausted, as he paced back and forth across the room. He had cut Mary Elizabeth down and put her on the couch. When the police asked Helen what had happened, she told them, and their eyes were incredulous.

"How could you get so angry over a little dirt?" one detective asked her.

"Angry? I wasn't angry," Helen replied. "I don't believe in anger. I told her what would happen, and it happened," she said.

The police, and some of the neighbors who had moved into the hall, stared at her in fascinated horror, and John stopped pacing, incomprehension written all over his face. "You understand, don't you?" Helen asked uncertainly, but she could see that they did not. She sighed, and the police grimly took her by the arm and led her out the door, shielding her from the neighbors, who had begun to look menacing.

It was a sensational case. During the relatively short trial the courthouse was packed with people, the newspapers ran thick black headlines, and neither Helen's lawyer nor the prosecutor could understand her attitude. She offered no defense whatsoever, and the psychiatrists were as puzzled as the legal experts. There seemed to be no real motive for the slaying other than Mrs. Taylor's repeated statement that she had told Mary Elizabeth what would happen if she got her dress dirty, and it had happened. She seemed to be, and the tests proved she was, completely rational. The neighbors testified they had heard nothing more than Mrs. Taylor rather sternly and resignedly calling Mary Elizabeth into the house just before the crime.

Mrs. Taylor's behavior at the trial was perfectly calm—the only peculiar thing was that she seemed genuinely puzzled that no one understood.

The result of the trial was predictable, under the circumstances. The State had a capital punishment law on the books, though it had seldom been invoked, and no woman had been executed under it in over a century. But when the jury filed into the courtroom after a short absence everyone knew what had to happen.

As the foreman stood up everyone fell into a hush that was absolute. John stared alternately at his wife seated at the table with her lawyer and at the judge, who asked Mrs. Taylor to rise and face the jury. Helen stood quietly as all eyes focused on the foreman. "How do you find?" the judge asked.

"We, the jury, find the defendant guilty of murder in the first degree, your honor," the foreman said in a cool, firm voice. "We recommend no clemency, and so say we all," he added and sat down.

The judge rapped twice on his bench as a murmur swept the courtroom. "So be it," he said. "Sentencing will occur immediately," and he turned to look down at Helen.

"Helen Taylor," he said, "the jury has found you guilty of one of the most heinous crimes ever to come before this court. Justice must take its course, and under the present conditions, there is only one course it can take. The law is clear, and it is inexorable and rational. For the deed you have committed the State demands the ultimate penalty. No mitigation or mercy can be shown to someone such as yourself. Society is dispassionate and just. You are hereby sentenced to be hanged by the neck until you are dead, date to be set subsequently by this court."

"Why, you do understand, after all!" Helen exclaimed as the judge adjourned the court and the babble drowned out her words.

"That's ridiculous," Fred says.

"And yet we do it all the time, don't we? What's the theme of the story?"

Fred furrows his brow. "That the death penalty is idiotic?"

"Good enough," the Author nods.

"Okay," Fred says slowly, leaning forward again. "I've thought of another question: besides character and theme, what are the other basic elements of a story?"

Plot and Atmosphere

"Well, there's plot, and there's atmosphere."

"Gimme, gimme," Fred says, wiggling the fingers of his left hand. "Don't keep making me pull it out of you."

"*Plot* has to do with the story line of actions and events that take place in the narrative, and the *resolution* of the conflict between protagonist and antagonist. Just as theme is the thread of thought that binds all elements of the narrative, plot can be defined as 'the thread of actions and events' that carries the narrative and that serves to exemplify the theme."

Fred scratches his head. "It's getting nice and cool in here," he says. "This antagonist—is it a person?"

"Not necessarily—it's whatever opposes the protagonist."

The Author stops typing to lean back and scratch his own head. Either Fred Foyle's action is catching, psychosomatically or otherwise, or the cats have been in his study again and there are fleas in the room. "But we need to discuss character a bit more first.

"Character has to do with the personal characteristics of the persons of the narrative—if we were writing a play we'd call them the cast, the *dramatis personae,* as the *Britannica* did. . . ."

"There go those foreign terms again. I think you writers like to use them because they make you feel superior." The author notices a sneer on Fred's physiognomy—

"See what I mean?" Fred shakes with sarcastic glee.

—on Fred's face. "Quit reading over my shoulder, will you?" the Author asks peevishly.

"I thought you said a writer's not supposed to use so many adjectives and adverbs to describe things," Fred says. "'Sarcastic,' 'peevishly.'"

"It's not a good idea to use lots, but a few won't hurt on occasion. But you're right—you ought to *show* it through action and dialogue, not *tell* about it with modifiers. But do you want me to answer your question about the elements of fiction or not?" There is a note of annoyance in the Author's voice.

"Shoot!" Fred says.

"Not a bad idea," the Author replies. "Anyway, it's the personal characteristics of the persons of the narrative that will determine their actions, reactions, and dialogue in any given situation. As I've said, the only necessary *persona*—that's a technical term we've used before meaning, in effect, 'a mask adopted by an author in order to tell a story'—is the *protagonist,* the main character of the story, the 'hero' or 'heroine.' However, a narrator may have a multiple protagonist—for instance, a group or a village—though normally one person will represent such a composite protagonist."

"Besides these personal characteristics, does a protagonist have any other qualities?"

"A protagonist will have two qualities, basically: a *dominant personality trait,* such as courage, generosity or fervor, and a *desire*—to *be,* to *have,* or to *do* something. This desire will aim the protagonist at an objective or *goal.*"

"I take it that the antagonist's purpose in the story is to block the protagonist from achieving the goal. Is that right?"

"Right again, Fred!" The Author beams at him, squinting into the screen of the monitor. "The protagonist will be blocked in his or her desire to attain his goal by a *logical* antagonist who may be another person in opposition; a situation, such as being lost in a blizzard; a force, as for instance society; or an aspect of the protagonist's own personality.

"This opposition of protagonist and antagonist leads to *conflict,* which is essential to the *dramatic situation*—be sure not to confuse this with the *dramatic viewpoint,* which has to do with the narrator, not the protagonist. This is the classic formula for a story: desire, opposition, conflict."

Viewpoint 2: Orientation, Person, Angle, Access

"I thought you said the narrator and the protagonist might be the same person?"

"But not always—in fact, not usually. An author has to choose a particular narrative viewpoint from which to tell the story, and here we're talking about *narrative voice*. A writer has several elements that must be combined in order to make up a narrative voice."

"As for instance . . . ?"

"First, there's *orientation*. There are two main choices to make here, and one secondary choice. From the *author-oriented* viewpoint, it is the author who narrates the story. From the *character-oriented* viewpoint, it is one of the personae in the story who narrates. The secondary choice is whether it's a major character—the protagonist or antagonist—who does the narration, or a minor character."

Fred nods. "So it's possible for the author of a story to be its protagonist as well, I take it."

"Yes, but if an author chooses that orientation he may be writing autobiography rather than fiction, and the fact that he's a character will have to take precedence. You'll see why when we get to *angle* and to *access,* which we've already mentioned in *viewpoint 1.* Right now, though, let's talk about the second element of viewpoint, *person.*

"The story may be narrated in the *first person*—that is, 'I went downtown that morning, had a bagel and coffee, and then went up to my office'; or in the *second person*—'You were sitting alone in your office that day when a tall blond walked through the door of your agency and sat down. "Hi, I'm Mike," he said.' This, though, is usually just a disguised form of *first person* narration. *Third person* narration is the most common of the three—'He took out a gun, aimed it carefully, and shot his own foot.'"

"Which he stuck in his mouth, like you did there." Fred begins to pace again. The attic room is cool at last. "I notice that when the blond walked in you used double quotes for his speech, but you used single quotes for the narration within your own speech, which was in double quotes."

Format and Punctuation 3

"Yes, that's the rule—double quotes, single quotes, double quotes, and so on *ad infinitum*. We've mentioned it before."

"You sure like that Latin," Fred says shaking his head.

"And then there's *angle*," the Author continues, ignoring him. "In the *single angle* only the actions of one character are followed; only what occurs in his or her presence is narrated. In the *multiple angle*—double, triple, etc.—what occurs in the presence of two or more characters is narrated. In the *omnipresent angle* the narrator has access to actions everywhere in the narrative."

"It would be hard for an author who made himself a character-narrator to tell the story from anything but the single-angle, wouldn't it?"

"Exactly, though it would be relatively easy to stand back from the story and tell it from the multiple-angle. Which brings us to *access:* the narrator may have only *objective access* to events; that is, he or she may narrate only actions observed externally. Or, the narrator may have *subjective access;* that is, she or he may be able to narrate not only external actions, but the thoughts and emotions of the characters as well."

"Things are getting complicated," Fred says.

"As with all other language techniques, the narrator may choose to blend any combination of orientation, person, access, and angle. The 'omniscient' viewpoint is a blending of narrative choices in which the author has joined omnipresent angle with subjective access to all characters—in other words, the author knows all about everything, internal and external, everywhere in the story, and narrates it that way."

"Let's see if I have this stuff down straight. The viewpoint of 'Savants' was character-oriented, first-person, single-angle, subjective-access narration."

"I couldn't have said it better myself, Fred."

"But what about 'Girl'? That had two voices. Does that mean that its viewpoint is author-oriented, third person, single-angle, objective access?"

"I think that's what you'd have to say."

"And *Heart of Darkness*?"

"That was frame narration, and it really has *two* points of view, I suppose you'd have to say. The narrator of the overall story is a minor character, so that's its orientation. He reports what Marlow says, describes the scene, and sets the mood, so the narration is third-person. There was only one scene, the yacht, and that's a single-angle. All the narrator knew was what the frame narrator told him, so he had only objective access."

"But the *real* story, about Mr. Kurtz, was told in a near-monologue, so you'd really have to double orientation, person, angle, and access, wouldn't you?" Fred asks, scratching his head. "Are there fleas in this room?"

"It's possible," the Author says. He scratches his stomach sur-reptitiously, bending forward toward the screen to hide his move-ments from Foyle.

"Have we covered all the basic elements of fiction now?" Fred raises his eyebrows inquisitively. Like his hair, they are pale, and they are lost for a moment in his forelock.

"Not quite. There's still *atmosphere,* and we haven't shown how dialogue can move the action—plot—along."

"Atmosphere . . . this is mood we're talking about now, I guess."

"Yes, and mood is created by means of the *setting*—the locale or environment in which the narrative takes place, the *attitude*—of the narrator and of the characters in the story, and *descriptions*."

"Some stories are all character, all plot, or atmosphere or even theme. Am I right?"

"Well, it can seem that way sometimes, but most stories will be a combination of all those things. Still, the fictionist may build the story by emphasizing any one or any combination of two or more of the four narrative elements: character, atmosphere, theme, or plot."

"So 'Savants' is a character story mainly. What's 'Girl'? I didn't get much of a sense of character, except maybe the toughness of the mother and a whiff of the innocence of the girl."

"What do you think it was?"

"A theme story?"

"Without a doubt, my fine Irish friend!"

"Okay, show me how dialogue can help set the scene and induce mood."

"Right. Here's some scene-setting in dialogue form from Ursula K. LeGuin's 'Conversations at Night'—it's the very opening of the story":

"The best thing to do is get him married."

"Married?"

"Shh."

"Who'd marry him?"

"Plenty of girls! He's still a big strong fellow, good-looking. Plenty of girls."

When their sweating arms or thighs touched under the sheet they moved apart with a jerk, then lay again staring at the dark.

"What about his pension?" Albrekt asked at last. "She'd get it."

"Fascinating!" Fred says, grinning. "Now, how about mood?"

"This is from H. G. Wells' novel *The First Men in the Moon*":

"If we were to set fire to all this stuff," I said, "we might find the sphere among the ashes."

Cavor did not seem to hear me. He was peering under his hand at the stars, that still, in spite of the intense sunlight, were abundantly visible in the sky. "How long do you think we have been here?" he asked at last.

"Been where?"

"On the moon."

"Two earthly days, perhaps."

"More nearly ten. Do you know, the sun is past its zenith, and sinking in the west? In four days' time or less it will be night."

"But—we've only eaten once!"

"I know that. And—but there are the stars!"

"But why should time seem different because we are on a smaller planet?"

"I don't know. There it is!"

"How does one tell time?"

"Hunger—fatigue—all those things are different. Everything is different. Everything. To me it seems that since first we came out of the sphere it has been only a question of hours—long hours. At most."

Fred clears his throat and says nothing for a moment. The two men listen to the sounds of the air conditioner until Fred breaks the stillness. "That's not just mood—and a strange one at that; it's setting, too," Fred says.

"The two go together, as theme goes with subject. Here's a whole atmosphere story":

The Man in the Booth

We didn't know he was dead until after the Gala was over. It was a small college-town fund-raiser for the Opera Association, and it was held on the stage of the college theater—on the stage itself, so that we could see the control booth, located at the rear of the auditorium, up where the balcony would have been in an old-fashioned place.

A number of tables had been set up on the stage, quite a number. There had been such a turnout that extra tables had to be found to accommodate the crowd, and some of us had to wait in the hall where Professor Hesse sat doling out the tickets and apologizing for the inconvenience. The musical director, Professor Malvolio, came out several times and asked when he could get the program going.

Finally, Hesse's table itself was commandeered, and the last of us were admitted and seated. The set, if it can be called that, consisted simply of three panels placed toward the front of the stage. There were large gaps separating them, and we could see between into the dark space where an audience would ordinarily have been listening. The seats rose in tiers into the blackness, those at the rear being only vaguely visible from the reflected light of the white spotlights that illuminated the set and the grand piano.

The program began at last with selections from "Brigadoon" sung by the Opera Chorus, which I enjoyed. I can't say the same for most of the rest of the program. I dislike opera, and I had decided to come at the last moment in order to accommodate my wife, who is employed by the Department of Music as record librarian. We were seated with the Bells—he is in the Department of Education, and she is one of my colleagues in the English Department, a former graduate student of mine, in fact—and some strangers who were the parents and grandparents of one of the performers, a graduate of the College who is studying now in New York City. My wife knew him. He sang an early solo in a small-town voice. He had no hope of becoming anything in the world of music, but it was clear he didn't realize it, for he postured like the imitation of a professional singer. It was while he was doing his number that my mind first began to wander and I noticed the man in the control booth.

Perhaps he was a student—it was hard to tell his age. The light in the booth was of that peculiar theatrical sort that seems to come from nowhere. It cast a dim illumination upon the top of his head so that only his hair and his facial prominences were visible—his nose, the cheekbones. For the rest of it, we could see the tops of his hands and arms when he rested them on the control panel. The light had a reddish cast, or perhaps that's only an impression. The only other light in the booth, behind the glass, was a single red dot in a piece of equipment that sat to his right, our left.

I can't say why he fascinated me so, but he did. I had some of the same sensations one experiences as one gazes into an aquarium. There were the thick glass, the same murky light seen in a fish tank at night if the radiance from a dim lamp is filtered through rusty, decaying vegetation. I used to sit in my parents' house when I was an adolescent, dreaming into my aquaria on the sun porch, the night outside lapping at the windows like dark water. Perhaps I would have looked, to a passer-by on the street, like an aquarian myself.

There was one truly outstanding voice in the Gala that evening. I don't know who he was—no program was published, and I didn't catch his name as Malvolio introduced him—but he clearly didn't belong in our town, though I gathered that he was indeed one of our citizens. He had a tremendous baritone and the looks to go with it.

I doubt that I've ever seen anyone who appeared more like an opera star. He was relatively young, dark-haired, with the countenance of a beardless satyr. In profile his face sloped like a cliff—interrupted by the outcropping of his Roman nose—to a slightly prognathous jaw. He took my attention entirely, and I stopped watching the booth. When the baritone was through singing the long intermission began.

The lights went up, and the cast of performers began to serve champagne to the guests. People began going to the buffet to pick up carved melon slices and grapes, cheese, celery stalks. My wife went forward while I sat and guarded the ladies' purses. Friends came by and we chatted. Eventually the lights blinked, people reseated themselves, and the evening's entertainment recommenced. My attention soon returned to the man in the booth.

I wondered why he was needed, for there were no microphones that I could see; the lights were set; anyone might have raised or dimmed the intermission lights when they were needed, yet there he sat through the whole performance, wearing headphones. Now and then he would smoke a cigarette, and its glow would intermittently blaze brighter than the red panel light to his right. Smoke rose in eddies through the viscous atmosphere behind the glass. Now and then he would move a bit, change his position.

When I was that young man dreaming away the evening in the sun porch, I could hear my father nearby, behind some bookcases that divided a third of the room into a study where he worked writing his sermons, which he would deliver on Sunday in the white clapboard church that stood next door. A lamp on one of the bookcases dropped its liquid glow onto his head and mine, though we could not see each other. Later, when I had left home, I would dream about that room of windows.

I would be seated before the aquaria. It would be night. The fish would be swimming in their dark waters, and as I watched, they would swim into the air of the room and maneuver about me. There was no boundary between surfaces and fathoms. I would look into the largest aquarium, trace the leaves of the rust-colored swordplant to its root, and there I would see my father's skull half-buried in the gravel, the stalk of the plant growing out of his eye.

It was not a pleasant dream, nor was it a nightmare. The emotions I felt were those of nostalgia and sorrow, of some sort of vague longing and regret. Still, I did not enjoy the dream's recurrence, and at last I exorcised it unwittingly by writing about it. I had not experienced that peculiar set of feelings again until the night of the Gala.

I can't say at exactly what point I began to notice that the man in the booth was motionless. He sat still in his chair while the voices and the piano flickered around us in the dim light. Now and then one of us leaned forward to whisper a comment into the ear of a companion. We nibbled pieces of fruit, sipped champagne. At last the chorus reassembled on the set to sing the grand finale, and the Gala was over.

The lights, however, did not go up. We sat in the semi-darkness applauding, until the applause began to seem labored and finally faded out. We began to murmur to each other in a subdued way, the sound watery, washing about us in eddies. Malvolio asked us in his harried manner to remain seated until he could get the lights on—"No sense in hurting ourselves on the way out, folks," he said. "I'll just send someone up to the booth to see what's wrong. I'll just be a minute. Wouldn't be a Gala if something didn't go amiss."

I saw him whisper to one of the performers, and after quite a long interval, during which some people got up and slowly made their way out anyhow, the lights went on.

Everyone laughed and got up, talking and gesturing. We began to make our way to the stage entrance where our coats hung on portable racks. I saw the performer return, and I noticed that there was something strange in his expression as he reported to Malvolio. The Director blanched and began to tremble. I asked my wife to wait for me in the hall, and I made my way toward Malvolio who was heading down the stage stairs and across the auditorium led by the young man who had been his emissary.

I caught up with them at the entrance to the control booth. Malvolio stuck his head into the doorway as the young man stood aside and stared blankly at me. I shouldered him aside and squeezed between the doorjamb and Malvolio. "My god," he said.

The man in the booth sat slouched in his chair, one arm resting on the control panel. The air was thick with smoke—one cigarette in the ash tray had burned down to the filter, and there was an acrid odor. The panel of dials glowed in the equipment. He still wore his headphones.

I looked outward through the window toward the stage. Beyond the set, through the gaps, I could see the last of the crowd moving stage right, toward the night outdoors. Hesse was acting as usher, urging the crowd forward discreetly as the performers, now serving as cleanup personnel, began clearing the tables in the wake of the dispersing audience.

Since we had been seated at one of the improvised tables farthest from the door, my wife and the Bells were among the stragglers. I could see them plainly. My wife appeared to be listening with only half an ear to Mrs. Bell, for she was looking toward the booth with a question written in her attitude. No doubt she could see me, too, if dimly, as I stood with Malvolio in the doorway behind the body of the man in the booth.

To my unpracticed eye, little appeared to be wrong with him. He sat with an air of relaxed attention. I could see his wavery reflection in the window—his eyes were open and dark. They stared into the empty theater, as though he were watching a play and waiting for his next cue. The heel of his hand rested on the counter, his fingers lying loosely around a lever. Beside his thumb, the only thing that looked out of place was an irregular pool of liquid that seemed as dark as the hours that rose in a tide outside the building and began to seep into the empty spaces of the receding Gala.

Rewriting

"I'm in an odd mood myself," Fred says, a note of anxiety, perhaps even of wonder in his voice. "Something just happened—what is it? It's as though something's missing and, simultaneously, as though I've experienced this before . . . sort of a combination of amnesia and *déjà vu*. What's going on?"

"I'm rewriting the manuscript, Freddy. Ten months have passed since you were born, and my editor wants me to add and cut. I just cut a whole story out of the manuscript, and now I've got to add material."

"What's your editor's name?—man, this is weird!" Fred avers.

"'Avers'? Fred asks, his lip curling, his brows raised. "You say I *aver* something?"

"See how those unusual verbs stick out? My editor's name is Nan."

"What does she want you to add?"

"Would you like to meet her?"

"Sure. How we going to do that?"

"By conjuring her up. Listen."

Fred cocks his head to the left so that his forelock flops down across the part in his hair which, though he is left-handed, is nevertheless on the left side of his head. He hears footsteps on the attic stairs, then a knock on the door.

"Come in!" the Author calls, pushing his rolling stool back

from the keyboard. The knob turns and Nan Deditter enters. She stands for a moment staring at the writer and the would-be writer *cum* foil.

"I'm surprised!" Fred whispers. "She looks more or less like a normal person. I thought editors were something like ogres in tiger's clothing."

"Shut up, Foyle!" The Author rasps, "She'll hear you. I don't know if that's what she looks like. It's how I imagine her." Turning to his fictive editor the Author rises and says in as gracious a manner as is possible for him, "Come in and sit down, won't you, Ms. Deditter?"

"Thank you," she replies. "Which of you is the Author?"

"I am, and this is my friend and partner, Fred Foyle."

"Oh, yes," Deditter says, smoothing the neatly pressed pleats of her linen skirt. "We've met."

"Do I detect a hint that she didn't like me?" Fred asks. He is speaking in a whisper still. His eyes are wide and staring. He is talking out of the side of his mouth.

"That's true, Fred, but you'll notice you're still around. I insisted on it."

Foyle says nothing but gives the Author a grateful glance before he focuses again on the editorial apparition.

"'Editorial apparition?'" both Foyle and Deditter exclaim simultaneously.

"Just checking to see if you're listening to me, both of you."

"What does she want you to do?" Fred asks.

"Please stop treating me as though I'm not in the room, Fred," Nan says evenly. "If I have reservations about your function in this book, they are based on a good deal of professional experience. All I want is for this book to be the best book on dialogue available in the market."

"Man, it's cold in here!" Fred says. He turns to shut off the air conditioner. "How long has this been running?"

"It's May now, not July. As far as you're concerned it's been running all fall, winter and spring."

"Okay, Nan," Fred says, addressing Ms. Deditter directly. "Then answer my question. What do you want him to do?"

"Besides get rid of you, you mean?" She cocks an eyebrow.

"I want him to write some effectively interactive dialogue," Nan says abruptly, addressing Fred. "Talk about why characters shouldn't make long speeches to one another, except in rare instances."

"You've done some of that," Fred says.

"I have to," the Author replies. "This is a didactic book, not a novel or a story, so this is one of those 'rare instances.' But it's true that characters shouldn't just stand around jawing, doing exposition and things like that."

"You mean like in 'Savants,' and 'Girl' and *Heart of Darkness*?" Fred asks.

Nan bristles. "They should avoid boring chat about the obvious and the trivial. Sometimes characters ought not to reply to one another directly, but obliquely or not at all, each one talking about his own preoccupation, and the like."

"Like I did just a while ago?" Fred asks the Author in a whisper still.

"Like you're doing right now," the Author says.

Fred clears his throat and turns his back on the room, staring out the window onto West Eighth Street where the maple is just beginning to look alive. "The trees are just starting to leaf out," he says. "Man, spring is sure late in this part of the country."

"I want you," Nan sits down on the La-Z-Boy and points a finger at the Author's chest, "to illustrate counterpoint in dialogue, the story's action moving back and forth from speaker to speaker, always moving, each speaker contributing something to the *whole*."

"How do you spell that?" Fred says, throwing a sharp glance back over his shoulder.

"Spell what?" Nan asks.

"Shut up, Fred. Nothing," the Author says. "Go on."

Fred shrugs. His head seems to sink into his shoulders. He doesn't move. "It's getting hot in here again," he says.

"I want you to show how characters react even when they're not speaking, showing that the other characters' comments are affecting them."

Fred turns the air conditioner back on. He leans over the rush of cool air and raises his arms slightly, so that the flow cools his chest and armpits. He casts a glance, full of distrust, back over his shoulder at his inventor and at his potential assassin.

Dialogue and Action

"Mmph!" the Author says to Nan. "You mean like this? This is a story titled 'Pleasant Dell.' It's about Horace, an old man bedridden in a nursing home":

Pleasant Dell

Horace lay in his bed and listened to the attendant shambling up the hall with the lunch cart. He heard Miller stop and unload one tray, knock once loudly on a door, then turn a knob and go in. A few moments later the squeaky wheels started up the corridor again. Eventually they got to Horace's room. By that time he was ready for Miller.

The knock was followed by a violent twist of the knob, and then a tray held by a thick, hairy arm was pushed through the doorway. Miller wore a white smock with short sleeves, jeans, and sneaks.

"Very ugly," Horace said as Miller deposited the tray on the night stand. "You, sir, are tremendously, not to say overwhelmingly foul of face and gross of limb." It had been a long sentence and Horace wheezed a bit.

"Who asked you?" Miller muttered at the old man. He turned around to leave.

But Horace stopped him. "Girls," he said.

"What?" There was a dog buried in Miller's throat. Horace could hear it snarling.

The hairs along the back of the old man's neck began to prickle with anticipation. He moved his long bones under the cold sheet, warped his lips into a malicious grin and said, "Girls, Miller. Girls, girls, girls. Young ones with big breasts and pearly round thighs. You got any?" He laughed. He caught himself, though, before he began to cough. The room rolled, but he focused at last on the huge attendant who stood, panting now, very close to the bed rail.

"I got girls," Miller said. "Lots." His knuckles swelled around the rail and began to turn white at the joints.

"Oh, verily. You have girls. Do they dance for you, Miller, flounce for you, jounce and bobble? How is it when you come to them in the night? Do their eyes glisten like the eyes of spring does in the moonlight? Ah, it must be sweet, you wag, the white flesh and its flailing in the shadows." The old man felt again, at last, the warm blood begin to stir in his toes, and the heart he'd listened for closely in the earlier white and quiet hours began to pump. There still is life, he thought—yes, still. It is still there.

Miller had grown darker. He loomed over the bed, his face thrust nearly into the gray stubble of Horace's beard. He seemed about to explode magnificently. His great lips twisted. "Nyarrgh!" Miller sounded, the whale word bursting out of his face. "Bloo bloo bloo! Ack, you old stink, blag, grah!" The childish and monstrous noises rocked him. He swayed on his feet, turned nearly purple.

"I'll kill you someday, by God I will." Then Miller seemed to collapse into himself, like a balloon on which someone had opened the valve.

The old man giggled in his sheets, his skin prickled and tingled. "Not someday, Miller," he said. "Now. Kill me now while I'm like this. I want to know I'm alive when I die, Miller." He felt it begin to ebb away. His lungs stopped heaving, and he looked up at the big man, his smile fading.

"No, not now. But I'll get you good one a these days. You'll see." He turned and went out of the room.

Horace lay and listened to the sound of the cart as Miller pushed it up the hall to the next door. It stopped, eventually started again, and at last it faded out of hearing. Horace remained listening. Silence settled down over the nursing home. It would be an infinite hour before the doctor and his nurse made their rounds.

The blood slowed in his veins, the sounds of the organs in their secret places diluted themselves with the pale buzzing of the electric clock on the bureau across the room, and Horace felt himself settle into wrinkles and fissures until he wasn't sure—he wasn't even sure that the ghost in the mirror so much as moved an eyelash.

Dr. Wiggins didn't even rap as he came in through the door, all bobbing spectacles and nodding goatee. Head Nurse Higgins rumbled along in his train, her thick legs chunking like wooden clappers inside the starched bell of her skirt, her ball-point pen puny in her stumpy fingers, her clipboard her insufficient shield.

Horace thought that Dr. Wiggins was much like the little mechanical canary his mother used to keep tucked away, years ago, in a closeted box. Now and then she would take it out, wind it up, and place it on the kitchen table. It would rock back and forth on its perch, in its raffia cage, and chirp metallically while ratchets whirred in the base beneath it. Horace remembered one morning in late spring when the bird had been gyrating on the table against the wall in front of the open window. Out of doors a lilac bush containing two sparrows had been filled with quarreling and bees, and the sun bloomed in the sky like some immense flower sprinkling its pollen over lawns and streets. Then, in the kitchen, the bird had stopped chirping, and for a moment there had been a pause in the morning. The sparrows had stopped their argument and listened, and then begun again. Horace's mother had smiled and wound up the bird some more. The act had seemed to go on and on, over and over until the day settled into evening and all the birds were stilled.

"Well, well, well, and how are we today?" Dr. Wiggins warbled.

"Well, well, well, and how is the famous vaudeville duo of Wiggins and Higgins today?" Horace retorted. "All right? We're all right in here. All zombies present and accounted for." Nurse Higgins glowered down at him. The doctor clucked and picked up the old man's wrist. "Pulse—zero," said Horace. "Normal." Then the stethoscope. "Heart—all quiet on the western front. Normal. Lungs—collapsed. Normal."

Dr. Wiggins set his lips, and Nurse Higgins rumbled in her throat as she jotted down his whispers. Then there was the shielded flashlight plunging into Horace's ears. "Brain—atrophied," Horace said. "Normal as hell."

"This is the part I like best," said the doctor. "It keeps him quiet for a minute." He took out a tongue depressor, forced it between two rows of brown teeth. Before his mouth was pried open Horace managed a single phrase, a slogan from an old Pepsodent toothpaste commercial: "You wonder where the yellow went?" And then he gagged as the flat stick came down hard on the root of his tongue.

"No sign of inflammation, Miss Higgins," the doctor said. "All seems in order at the moment. Regular medication. Congratulations, Horace.

You've made it through another twenty-four hours." The old man detected more than a bit of annoyance in Wiggins' voice. He felt the doctor's fingers relax on the depressor, and quite deliberately Horace brought his jaws together, catching the tip of a middle finger between his incisors.

Dr. Wiggins cursed, his eyeballs bulging bloodily through his lenses, and jerked his hand away. Horace laughed. "Feels good to get some solid food again," he said. The nurse was poised on her toes, as though she meant to jump on him. Her little black mustache trembled. "Come ahead, girly," Horace offered, raising a knotted hand and crooking his finger at the woman. "It's been a long time. . . ." He was cut short by her furious assault on his bedclothes.

She pulled the top sheet down hard and tucked its trailing flap expertly under the mattress. The sheet was so tight across his chest that Horace had to struggle to breathe. Next, she tore the pillow out from under him—his head bounced hard on the taut undersheet—and fluffed it as though she were punching a bag. She jerked his head up and stuck the pillow back into place. She stood breathing heavily, her nostrils flaring like a mare's.

"You're the worst patient we've ever had here at Pleasant Dell," the doctor said, "and we've had some pips. You're a vicious old man. Perhaps where you're going next you'll learn civility." The doctor spun and left. Nurse Higgins followed, slamming the door.

The room jolloped and skittered around as Horace lay trying to make the walls stand still. The portrait of the Governor beside the white-draped window dripped its vacuous smile down the drawn shade.

The ceiling snowed into the mirror like a plaster blizzard. The yellow tiles of the floor rippled and rolled. At last things settled down and Horace could ponder Dr. Wiggins' parting salvo. Going? Am I dying, then, at last? Horace asked the slight mound that swelled his sheets. No, that couldn't be it; the examination had been normal. Nothing was wrong there. Then what could it be? He lay wondering until suppertime. The excitement felt good. He almost regretted it when he heard Miller coming with his meal.

"Hi ho, Miller, my fine lad," he said when the attendant at last stood at his bedside, "what news?" Miller put the tray down next to the old one, scarcely touched, left over from lunchtime. Often Miller, who was supposed to pick up the trays after the one-o'clock examination, left them until he came around again in the evening. He could usually expect a cutting comment or two about it from Horace, so he glared down now, suspicious of his tormentor's unexpected joviality.

"No news," Miller growled. "We're moving tomorrow, is all."

"Moving? What do you mean, my fellow?"

The word *fellow* increased Miller's suspicion, so he answered very guardedly. "Going to the new place, just been built."

Horace hated the little flecks of saliva that collected at the corners of Miller's mouth. He looked away and said, "Leaving! But why?"

Miller had been about to leave, but he stopped. "Ain't you heard? The State condemned this place. Bad wiring and fire escapes. So we're going to a new place, just been built on the other side a the property. Tomorrow."

Horace didn't answer. Miller turned, his shoulders slumping in relief. His hand was on the knob when it came, the magic word, rebounding softly off the white surfaces of the room and settling into the corners muskily.

"Girls. Soft, round, bottomy girls, all pink and pearl, opening like sweet night flowers in the twilight, Miller. You got any? Bring me some, Miller, the ones you can't use and don't want. Pluck me blossoms, big lad. Leaves and loves—all the dusky women you don't need."

Miller screamed. Like a cat, his voice clawed around the room and down the corridors of Pleasant Dell. He crouched and leaped, his knee ringing on the iron rail as he landed in the bed, weeping and tearing. "Kill me, Miller," Horace managed to gasp, grinning, as the big knuckles settled around his neck and darkness began to tingle up through the rushing arteries. Footsteps and voices, and other hands twisting Miller's claws loose before the inner blackness closed with the pressing and sterile white of the walls.

Horace could tell it was morning when he awoke, by the quality of the light on the shade over the window. His door was open into the hallway. As Horace came to and began to watch, he saw Nurse Higgins pass his door trundling a wheel chair which contained Mrs. Jennison, the inmate of the room next to his. She was followed by another nurse who propped old Mr. Peters with one arm as he tottered along leaning on his cane. Then there came Miller with Sally Snell and several others of the inhabitants of Pleasant Dell who were able to make the journey to and down the stairs under their own power.

For three-quarters of an hour or so there was activity of this sort, and then it ceased. Horace waited expectantly for a while, and then he began to fret. "When the hell—," he started. And then he heard more voices and footsteps. It was the movers.

They began at the foot of the hall and worked their way up, room by room, until they reached Horace's door. The old man could hear Dr. Wiggins directing things, and then he appeared in the doorway. He stood there in profile for a moment, saying something to one of the moving men, and then he pulled the door to.

Stunned, Horace lay in bed quietly, and then slowly he began to struggle into a sitting position. When at last he sat leaning against the headboard he was panting heavily and his heart was racing. He was alert—so alert that he could hear every sound the movers made as they gutted the rooms all around his. By the time they had finished their work the old man was exhausted, and the room was beginning to tilt at odd angles again. A voice—he barely recognized it as his own—said, "They can't be going to leave me!"

It was a hollow voice, and it made a hollow sound in the empty building. "They can't be going to make me go this way, listening to my insides fade like a lily." But there was no one to answer him, and no other sound except the humming clock on the bureau. And then that, too, stopped as somebody somewhere cut the current.

Horace had no idea how long he had sat there in light and dusk, listening and dreaming, until he heard the faint sounds coming from the head of the stairs. When he was sure he actually had heard them, though they had now ceased, he called out. There was no response.

Panic glutted him, and then, with a movement so fast it surprised him, he threw back the sheet and forced his feet over the edge of the bed. It was too fast. Vertigo seized him and he nearly fell to the floor. But finally he managed to steady himself and force the room to stand still. Then he eased himself off the bed and stood shakily erect. The nightshirt fell loosely to his knees, and he was amazed at first to realize that those two frail white spindles were actually holding him upright. Carefully, he moved toward the door. He had almost made it when his knees buckled and he fell heavily. He lay on the yellow tiles. "Oh, God, God," he said, though he hadn't believed in God in fifty years and more. He didn't hear the door swing back, but when he opened his eyes he saw the dirty sneakers.

Miller bent down and then squatted, folding his arms over his knees. Horace saw the jaw swinging there like a ledge when he raised his head. "Miller!" he said. And then he remembered Miller's promise.

"Miller, how's the girls?" Horace asked.

"There ain't no girls," the ledge said. "You know that. They left me behind, too. Come on, we can still catch up."

Horace felt a big arm lift him like a twig and set him on his feet. Then, somehow, Horace felt strong enough to walk. The two men went down the hall, down the stairs, and out of the door onto the long lawn of Pleasant Dell. Night was falling over the old mansion and its acres of land, and over the forest that fringed the grounds.

"Why are you helping me, Miller?" Horace walked steadily now, if not firmly, with the young man's arm circling his back.

"I dunno," Miller said. "Everybody's got to have some place to go. We can still catch up. They went this way, into the woods."

Night fell darkly as they entered the first trees. Horace noticed the birds first as they stopped singing. He could no longer see the way, but crickets took up the chorus in the underbrush, and there were spring toads noting shadows as Miller led him deeper into the forest where, faintly, Horace heard a sound like a mechanical canary running down.

"Holy smokes!" Fred exclaims. "What a beginning!" He looks directly at Nan Deditter. "Is that 'interactive dialogue'?"

Nan stares back at him but says nothing. At last Fred drops his eyes and says something under his breath. He looks up when he hears the attic door slam shut and feet stuttering down the stairs. He shifts his gaze to the Author, his eyes asking a silent question.

"She'll probably be back." Fred's mouth begins to open. "Don't say it. She knows everything you do, whether she's in the room or not." Fred Foyle sits quietly for a moment or two riffling the pages of the manuscript that have so far been run off on the laser printer.

"Well, that sure was dialogue moving the action along, all right."

"But I didn't have to use it as an example, because we'd already done interactive dialogue."

"When?"

"When I brought Nan into the study. Go back and look it over." The Author leans against the soft back of his typing stool, stretches, and glances at his watch.

"Are we about through with dialogue as it applies to the elements of the short story?"

"Just about. I'm ready for a break. How about you?"

Viewpoint 3: Subjective, Objective, Dramatic

"Oh, sure, sure," Fred says, pushing his wayward forelock back into his hairline.

"Tell you what—while I'm gone, you can fool around with the computer if you like. Can you type?"

"I think so." Fred looks dubious.

"Well, go ahead and give it a try. I'll be back in about ten." The Author rises and leaves, wishing immediately that he hadn't—the heat on the attic stairs outside the door is like a big fuzzy mitten enveloping his body. As he goes carefully down the steep stairs he hears the soft clicking of the keyboard behind him.

"I thought he'd never leave," Fred writes. "Sure, I can type— whatever he can do, I can do as well or better. This business of being Fred Foyle is a drag. Why couldn't it have been I who am the Author instead? I could have invented him instead . . . no, I'd have invented somebody else, just to get even . . . only, if I were the Author and he weren't invented, how could I get even with him? Man, this is getting too philosophical for a book on how to write dialogue. Let's keep it simple.

"Okay, let's see, what am I writing now? It must be a monologue—no, I'm thinking it, not speaking it aloud, so it's got to be a soliloquy: 'To be, or not to be—*that* is the question!' Only I've got no choice in the matter. I've been created and that's that. . . ."

"You're no worse off in that regard than anybody else," the Author says. Fred jumps.

"Good grief!" he gasps, "I didn't hear you come in. Don't sneak up on me like that again, okay?" Fred slides off the stool and the Author takes his place, leaning over the keyboard and squinting at the monitor.

"Let's see what we've got here," he says, scrolling back to what Fred has written.

"It's a soliloquy," Fred says.

"It's more than that. On the surface, it looks like an example of subjective voice."

"Fred leans over the Author's shoulder and looks. "Did you do that on purpose?" he asks. "Leave the room, I mean. Did you figure I'd write something like that?"

"Sure," the Author says.

"That's pretty manipulative."

"Of course. What do you think you're here for?"

Viewpoint 4: Aspects of Narration

Fred makes a strangling noise in his throat, pauses, and then he says, "So that's the subjective voice?"

"From your perspective it is. You see that there's only one aspect of narration. Your point of view is the only one in the soliloquy."

"What other point of view can there be?"

"Well, think of yourself—a persona, an invented character—standing in the center of a circle . . . that's your world. Now also imagine a narrator standing off to one side, outside the circle, looking at it—the character's world—and at the character *in* that world. Now, imagine that the narrator begins to tell what's going on with the character. He or she is using the *objective voice,* and this perspective has two aspects. The reader sees what's happening to the character—that's the *aspect of narration.* and the reader also gets a sense of how the narrator feels about the character by the manner in which the narrator tells the story, makes the persona act and speak—that's the second aspect, the *aspect of reflection.*"

"You mean whether the narrator tells the story humorously, or seriously, or whatever?"

"Right. Take that last story. We know that Horace is, in a way, a humorous figure, by the way in which he talks and acts, but we also know that the humor has an edge to it—it's a *black humor*. We also know that Miller is a limited and sullen person, whom Horace can manipulate at will because he's smarter. We feel sorry for Miller, but possibly we feel even sorrier for Horace. When one uses the objective voice one may be telling one's own or someone else's story, but telling it by standing off at a distance. Even so, the reader is not excluded from the story because we see the speaker reflected in the way the author tells the story."

"Are you saying that if somebody discusses true feelings and bluntly states opinions and ideas, that's something other than fiction?"

"Right, Fred. That's *subjective viewpoint*. The reader may be excluded."

"But if an author tells what really *happened* to him or her, that *is* a story?"

"Exactly, but if it's a true story it's autobiography, not fiction. Still, it's *objective viewpoint*.

"But Shakespeare wrote plays, so that's not 'objective voice' or 'subjective voice,' is it?"

"No, you're right. When we discussed orientation, person, angle, and access we were breaking down objective voice into its components, but Shakespeare was going one step further—he was using *dramatic voice*. That is, he put on a mask—he *became* his character and we know that character's world from the inside, just as we know a subjective speaker's perspective. But we don't have to talk about Shakespeare and drama, we can talk about some stories we've read or discussed."

Fred nods, but without conviction. "You mean like 'Savants' and 'Girl'?"

"And even *Heart of Darkness*. Think of it this way: You have your circle, and you have your character standing in the center of that circle; you have your narrator standing off to one side. But the narration pierces the circle instead of stopping outside it—the narrator enters the mind and body of his or her character, makes the character act, think, and speak. So you have the aspect of narration; and you have the subjective aspect of the character, and then you have the aspect of reflection because we know how the narrator feels about the character by the way in which the character is manipulated."

"So subjective voice is *exclusive* because it has only one aspect; objective voice is *inclusive* because it has two aspects—narrative and reflective, but dramatic voice is *most inclusive* of the three because it has a third aspect . . . the subjective aspect *from the character's point of view*?"

"You've got it, Fred."

"So what I wrote up above is subjective voice?"

"From your point of view, yes."

"Is the tip-off of subjective voice the pronoun '*I*'?"

"At first glance it might appear so, but in fact, the dramatic voice uses 'I' too: 'I, Horace, would like to die violently so that I know I'm alive and not already dead when I die.' That's why your soliloquy is dramatic voice and not subjective voice, because it was spoken by a character I invented, not by the Author."

Fred is silent for a moment. The Author can see him flushing with frustration, resentment, embarrassment, chagrin—or a combination of all those emotions. "So there's no way I can write anything subjectively?"

"No way in the world." The Author shakes his head ruefully. "I'm sorry, pal. You're almost purely dialogue."

"But what's the point of it all?" Fred asks. His tone is rueful, too. "Why get so complicated with piling subjective voice upon objective voice upon dramatic voice upon frame narration? I mean, why should a story have to be so complicated?"

"It doesn't *have* to be complicated, but if an author wants texture and depth, then the more aspects of narration that are included the thicker the texture will be, and the deeper the mood will plunge. *Heart of Darkness* is a classic of brooding depth and moody texture, and much of that effect is the direct result of narration by one character listening to the monologue of another. The more inclusive a story is, the better the chance that it will mirror the world."

"Forget it," Fred says. "Let's go on to something else."

Foreshadowing

"No, let's do some summing up. We've considered dialogue as it applies to the four basic elements of fiction; that is to say, character, setting/atmosphere, plot, and theme, but we haven't mentioned some of the things dialogue can do and shouldn't do with regard to these subjects. For instance, dialogue can be used as a foreshadowing device."

"That means 'giving a hint of things to come,' doesn't it?"

"Exactly. Can you think of a place where that's happened in one of our examples?"

Fred lowers himself slowly to the seat of the La-Z-Boy and perches on the edge of it. He looks sleepy. He rubs the back of his right hand with his left. "Got it!" he says, snapping his fingers. "How about in 'Pleasant Dell' where Miller says—let's see—" he leafs through the issue of *The Carleton Miscellany* where it originally appeared, "'I'll kill you someday, by God I will.' Is that a place?"

"A rather blatant example, indeed, but yes, it is."

"But he doesn't do it."

"Doesn't he?"

Fred looks bewildered.

"Well, what happens at the end of the story? Never mind, you can think about it when you're off duty."

Dialogue and Moralizing

"When I'm 'off duty' I'm nowhere, pal," Fred sneers. "Do you know where 'nowhere' is? It's nowhere, limbo, nada, Erewhon.

When you dismiss me," he gestures emotively with his skinny arm, "I become one with the cosmos, my ego disappears, I come to the end of the sevenfold path to Nirvana. I can take no magazines there—I can't even take *myself* there. You continue with your humanity, but I enter the fogs of the Underworld and wander betwixt Styx and Lethe!"

"Thanks."

"Thanks? Thanks for what?" Fred asks.

"For illustrating overemphasis on theme. Dialogue can, in Nan Deditter's words, 'drive the special nails that fasten a story's meaning down solidly,' but as she points out also in this letter of . . . let's see, nuts! I can't find the first page. Well, anyway, she also points out that there can be 'overkill in this respect, blatant moralizing.' That was real blatant, Fred."

"Glad to be of service," Fred moans. He sits down again. "What's next? What else can I do for you? Man, how I hate this!"

The Author cocks an eyebrow at Fred, who catches the irony in the gesture. "Forget I said that," he says.

"Here's some more foreshadowing," the Author says, "in a passage that contains interactive dialogue, internal monologue—all sorts of things we've been talking about. It's from the science-fiction novel *Dune* by Frank Herbert":

How many times must I tell that lad never to settle himself with his back to a door? *Hawat cleared his throat.*

Paul remained bent over his studies.

A cloud shadow passed over the skylights. Again Hawat cleared his throat.

Paul straightened, spoke without turning: "I know. I'm sitting with my back to a door."

Hawat suppressed a smile, strode across the room.

Paul looked up at the grizzled old man who stopped at a corner of the table. Hawat's eyes were two pools of alertness in a dark and deeply seamed face.

"I heard you coming down the hall," Paul said. "And I heard you open the door."

"The sounds I make could be imitated."

"I'd know the difference."

He might at that, *Hawat thought*. That witch-mother of his is giving him the deep training, certainly. I wonder what her precious school thinks of that? Maybe that's why they sent the old Proctor here—to whip our dear Lady Jessica into line.

"That foreshadowing is subtler," Fred Foyle says, "but it's all mixed in with exposition, characterization, plot development, and scene-setting."

"Right," the Author says. "I thought it might make a pretty good summary of this section."

"And so it does," says Fred. "Why don't we call it a day?"

"Let's call it a chapter, too," the Author replies as he pushes the keys to save his file and exit from the word-processing program. "Get a good night's sleep."

"No, wait!" Fred yells, but it's too late.

Chapter 3

Diction

"So *there* you are!" Fred exclaims as the Author boots the computer, logs onto his program and accesses his file. "What took you so long? Where've you been?"

The Author blinks vacantly at the screen and yawns. "I took the Memorial Day weekend off. The weather was just beautiful and I didn't feel like being stuck in this garret while everyone else was off at the beach."

"Everybody but me," Fred says.

"That's the way it goes. You can't win 'em all."

"Got any more clichés to ply me with?" Fred asks through a curled lip. He brushes the hair out of his eyes. "What are we gonna talk about now?"

"A whole bunch of things, all of them related."

"Such as?"

"Syntax, diction, and style, for three, and then dialect and slang."

"We've talked about some of those things before."

"No," the Author says, shaking his head. "We've mentioned them, but we've not discussed them, and they're important. Not only are they related to and supportive of one another, they are also directly related to viewpoint, which we've just finished discussing. We need to begin by doing some defining," the Author says.

"You never get tired of doing that, do you?" Fred sighs.

Syntax 1: Subjective Word Order

It's how we know things, Fred. Naming something is a basic human step in the acquisition of knowledge." It's the Author's turn to sigh. "Donald Davie in a 1958 book called *Articulate Energy* talked about the three traditional types of syntax or 'word order' in the sentence. He pointed out that, with regard to *subjective syntax,* word order follows the 'form of a thought' in the mind of the writer."

"Do we have an example of subjective syntax?"

"If you were a real person we would have had an example at that spot where I left the room and you began to compose on the computer. We saw, however, that what you wrote was really from the dramatic viewpoint because I was putting words into your mouth, into the mouth of an invented persona. However, since I am a real person . . ."

"Don't rub it in," Fred says bitterly.

". . . an example of subjective syntax would be, 'I, the Author, am quite proud of my invented character Fred Foyle."

"Aw, shucks," Fred says, a blush staining his pale features.

"And that's exactly what I have against Fred," Nan Deditter says.

Both Fred and the Author jump.

"Oh, my soul!" Fred says, panting and holding a hand to his thin chest, as though to keep the heart from bursting through his shirt.

The Author composes himself. "What soul, Fred?" he asks. Then, "We didn't hear you come in, Nan. Have a seat. What are you talking about?"

"I'm talking about Fred Foyle and why I would have liked you to get rid of him." Nan Deditter touches her hair and sits down on the La-Z-Boy. "Your strategy in this book is certainly unusual and imaginative, setting up the whole book as a dialogue between yourself as author and a fictional character, Fred Foyle. However, I don't believe it has precisely the effect you intended. Despite his many charms as a character, and despite the originality of your concept, I don't think Fred's helping the book."

The look on Fred's face is heart-rending, the Author thinks. To Nan he says, "What on earth are you talking about?"

"One problem with this strategy," Nan replies, "is that you end up talking, in effect, to yourself: to your own personal straight man, your ventriloquist's dummy whom you can make understand, applaud, be impressed, or be satisfied with explanations, whenever you find it convenient he should."

"Let me get this straight, Nan," the Author says, leaning forward. "In other words, you object that Fred is a 'fictional character,' yet what I am supposed to do in this book is teach novice writers how to manipulate *their* fictional characters, invent speeches for them, make characters do what the novices want them to do—in other words, you chastise me for doing what you want me to teach my students to do! Is that right?"

"Fred does nothing to curb an inclination to 'point and move' style: as soon as he says everything's clear, you move on . . . and he says it's clear whenever you want him to."

"So what? If Fred weren't in the book, I'd still move on when I figure I've made something clear."

"As long as you're talking to Fred, a character who simply wants to *understand,* you're *not* talking to the reader, who needs not only to understand, but to *do.* The reader needs, not only to intellectually *learn* the principles discussed by you and embodied in the examples, but also needs to be able to *apply* those principles independently in his or her own fiction. Fred Foyle has no such needs."

"I object!" Fred cries, jumping to his feet. "I'm as ambitious as anybody. I wouldn't be asking these questions if I didn't want to be a writer myself. I say so right from the beginning. I'd like to be the Author—in fact, I *am* the Author, as you yourself point out."

Nan ignores him, but she continues to talk about Fred as though he were a real third person, distinct from the Author. "His strongest interest is apparently purposeless curiosity," she continues, "as contrasted with a reader's urgent need for guidance in some-thing he's already engaged in doing: that is, writing fiction. So Fred is meaningfully unlike the reader to whom the book is ad-dressed and therefore does not serve well as a surrogate for him. I'm afraid, at some points, the happy cross-chat with Fred will leave the reader unsatisfied, feeling he's merely overhearing talk that's not really directed to him or his concerns, lacking the guid-ance for which he bought the book in the first place."

"Hold it right there, Nan!" the Author cries, pawing through his correspondence. "Here it is!" he cries triumphantly. "Let me read you something you wrote to me. One of the subjects you want me to cover is, and I quote, 'Using dialogue (as opposed to summary narration) to increase immediacy and the readers' feel-ing that events are moving quickly right before their eyes. The in-creased reader involvement of "eavesdropping" on dialogue rather than passively having the author tell you, the reader, about some-thing, all tidy and predigested. Keeping an effective balance between dialogue and other storytelling elements.' You can't have it both ways," the Author points out. "If my talking with Fred doesn't give the reader a sense that he or she is eavesdropping on a conversation rather than reading a schoolbook, then what *does* it do?" He pauses. Nan says nothing.

"I'll tell you what, Nan," the Author continues, "I'll write an Introduction in which I'll answer some of these questions. Will that help?"

Nan pays no attention. She is either so absorbed in what she is saying that she doesn't hear the Author, or she is not physically present in the room to hear him. "It's really crucial that this book be solid, reader-friendly, reader-conscious how to, not academic overview, as it sometimes now seems. Assuming that's not the im-pression you wanted to make, can I persuade you to reconsider using Fred and talk to the reader instead?"

The Author thinks for a moment. Fred is beyond thinking. He simply sits at the Author's trestle desk with his mouth hanging open and his eyes faintly crossed, glazed over. At last the Author leans forward to reply.

"Nan, I am the son of a Baptist minister. I had to go to church every Sunday and be preached at. I didn't like it. As a teacher, I don't like books that preach at me, telling me *how* I'm supposed to do things. I am committed, however, to teaching my students *how* they can approach writing, and I give them all a range of techniques that are to be found in most fiction, though not every piece of fiction (or poetry or drama) will use all those techniques. I try to invent strategies that will *engross* my students." He pauses to shake his head in a rueful manner. "Forgive me if I'm obtuse," the Author resumes, "but I can imagine no strategy more likely to succeed in teaching dialogue writing than writing a whole book in dialogue form. I'm sorry, I realize your argument is sincere, but I don't believe you're correct. I'm going to keep Fred."

Fred turns but, quick (and grateful) as he is, he is not fast enough to catch Nan Deditters's departure. "My God!" he says, "that was awful! What was it all about?" He is even paler than usual.

"It was all about *subjective syntax,* personal opinion."

"Was she really here?"

"In the flesh, no; in her words, yes. That's just how she felt about you, Fred, fourteen years ago. I invented nothing. Those were all quotes. Did you notice how the word order of each of her written sentences expressed *as exactly as possible* the train of thought going through her mind? That is subjective syntax."

"Wait! Wait!" Fred shouts. "What do you mean 'fourteen years ago'?"

"Well, those were Nan's opinions while I was writing this book in 1988. It's 2003 right at the moment. I retired from teaching writing arts in 1996, seven years ago. You and I no longer live in upstate New York. We're in Maine now."

Fred is clearly astounded. "But I don't feel any different," he says.

"You haven't aged, Fred, but I have. My office is in an old barn now, and I'm typing this book into my latest computer, a Mac G4, though my original computer, an Osborne 1, is upstairs in the loft, and it still works, I think."

Fred is silent. He's obviously considering things. "Was our book published?" He gives the Author a straight look.

"Yes, in 1989."

"How did it do? Was Nan right? Do people hate it?"

The Author nods. "She was partly right. Some people do seem to dislike it, but so far the book has sold over 50,000 copies in several editions and many printings."

"Holy cats!" Fred breathes. "But who *doesn't* like it?

"Well, it's been reviewed on the Web by ordinary readers, and some of them hate it as much as Nan Deditter did. But there's something odd about that."

"What do you mean, odd?"

"Almost all of the negative reviews were written by women." Silence fills the barn. Then Fred says, "You're kidding."

The Author shakes his head. "No. That's an actual fact."

"What do you make of it?"

"I don't. And I'm going to leave it at that."

Syntax 2: Objective Word Order

Having recovered to a degree, Fred asks, "How about the second kind of syntax?"

"With regard to *objective syntax,* word order follows a 'form of action' in the world at large. We must have some examples of that kind of syntax somewhere. Let's see—" the Author riffles through the completed portion of the manuscript. "You know," he says, "there really isn't much here. Almost everything so far is dialogue. Oh . . ." he says, "I think I've got one. Yes, it's from the opening of 'Pleasant Dell': 'Horace lay in his bed and listened to the attendant shambling up the hall with the lunch cart.'"

"So objective word order in effect just lays out an action on the page?"

"Exactly. Here's another example, from the first paragraph of 'Hardware,' a short story by Lester Goldberg, told from the character-oriented, first-person, objective, single-angle viewpoint":

The football spiraled into the sky. I cut right, leaped and grabbed it, tucked it in, ran a few steps, then turned toward my father and lobbed the ball back. Cut right, cut left: he threw pass after pass. As the sun dropped behind the factory roof and the Pyrene Fire Extinguisher sign glowed red, we knew my mother could see it from our apartment and it was time to head for home. On the way, walking a few feet apart, I still had to be alert—my father might pop the football at me underhanded.

"Question," Fred says. "Do you remember that passage you quoted from Christopher Isherwood's novel *The Memorial*?"

"Yes, of course."

"Well, there was a section that read like this: 'And then she'd ask him about the office and whether the work was very hard and how he liked it. And he began to tell her, carefully and seriously, suddenly breaking off. . . . '"

"What about it?" the Author asks.

"Those sentences are *describing dialogue*. Is that objective syntax?"

"Absolutely. In fact, if I had kept going with the paragraph from Lester Goldberg's story, we'd have seen some of it:

He told me about his dream backfield: Marshall Goldberg, Pittsburgh Panthers halfback; Sid Luckman, Chicago Bears, quarterback; Paul Robeson, Rutgers, fullback. Two Jews and a Negro.

"A person speaking is performing an action, and the description of a speech is bound to be written in objective word order."

"Then what syntax is used in speech itself?" Fred asks.

Syntax 3: Dramatic Word Order

"The third type of syntax discussed by Davie is *dramatic syntax:* word order follows the 'form of thought' in the mind of a persona invented by the writer."

"I don't suppose we need to provide too many examples of that sort of syntax," Fred notes. "We have tons of that—almost everything in this book, I suppose."

"Especially in the monologues by the men in the *Bordello*."

"That's something I've been wanting to ask," Fred says with a quizzical look in his eye. "Why in the world did you write those poems?"

"When I got my first teaching job," the Author says, thinking back, "I was required to teach novels about all these 'fallen women,' *Tess of the d'Urbervilles; Maggie, a Girl of the Streets; The Scarlet Letter*. It annoyed me that the point-of-view of the men involved was scanted. So I sat down at my desk in Cleveland (at the time) and tried to rectify the situation. To make it as tough on myself as possible, I decided I was going to use some difficult verse forms as well."

"Your first teaching job?" Fred asks. "That was a while ago."

"Yes."

"Why didn't you use something more current? Haven't you written anything like it since?"

"A whole book of interactive monologues titled *The Green Maces of Autumn, Voices in an Old Maine House,* that came out in 2002."

"Why didn't you use those?"

"Because a printmaker, George O'Connell, turned all the *Bordello* poems into a beautiful portfolio of poem-prints which was published and exhibited at an art gallery in Albany, New York, in 1996. That's pretty current. I even added another poem to the set, 'Tom Biggins.'"

"How did you manage to get anybody to exhibit something with a title like that?"

"There was no problem in Albany," the Author says, "in fact, it was a women's college there that exhibited them. Unfortunately, my *alma mater,* the University of Connecticut, wasn't as large-minded. They banned it."

Fred was impressed. "You've written a banned work?" He and the Author did a high five. "Way to *go*!"

Diction 3: Levels of Diction

"Right. Now, Fred, I suppose you've noticed that these kinds of syntax have parallels with the 'voices' we discussed much earlier—subjective, objective, and dramatic voices. There are other parallels as well—with *diction*.

"In contemporary speech, this sentence would be an example of normal word order: 'A thought of grief came to me alone.' The subject comes first, then the predicate 'A thought/came to me. . . . ' In line four of stanza three from Wordsworth's poem 'Ode: Intimations of Immortality . . . , ' this normal syntax is changed: 'To me alone there came a thought of grief.' The two sentences say exactly the same thing, but they *sound* different because of the syntax, which has transformed the *level* of diction in the line. The tone of the second version has been 'elevated.'"

"Is there a one-to-one relationship between syntax and diction?" Fred asks.

"No," the Author replies, shaking his head, "but they are related. They depend on one another, but they are not the same thing. Syntax is concerned with the *form* of the sentence; diction has to do with its *tone* and *style*. The level of diction of a truck driver is usually different from that of an archbishop." The Author pauses a moment and looks down at the pile of books scattered on the attic floor behind him. He returns his gaze to the monitor and commences typing again.

Tone and Style 1: High, Mean, Base

"An archbishop speaks in an elevated 'style,' a truck driver, perhaps, in an idiomatic or slangy style. These styles are dependent on the levels of diction in which the individuals choose to speak.

"For instance, a truck driver in a play or story could not say, 'To me alone there came a thought of grief' because the sentence wouldn't be in character; the level of diction is lofty, not vernacular. To be believable as a character, the truck driver would have to say something like, 'A sad thought came to me by my lonesome.' The level of diction would then be in keeping with the character, and the sentence would be an example of *base* style."

"Give me another example of base style," Fred says.

"Okay, take this sentence from one of my pieces titled, 'The Bo'sun's Story': 'I'd went upstairs early that night when my pa come home drunk.' That's base style and a low level of diction. A more ordinary level would have been, 'I'd gone upstairs early that night when my father came home drunk.' But the bo'sun can't say that because it would have been out of character. He's a career sailor aboard a Navy ship. He's had little education. A yeoman—a Navy clerk—who might have more education, could have said it the second way."

"I see," Fred says. "So if an older, well-educated woman character were written into the script of our hypothetical play, she might have said, 'A thought of grief came to me alone,' right?"

"Exactly. That would be mean style. The archbishop might say, "To me alone there came a thought of grief'—high style and elevated diction. Only in this last version, however, is the word order, the syntax, out of normal order. It is 'artificial' syntax and it doesn't seem 'natural,' but it is perfectly good English.

"Let me recapitulate. There are three voices: subjective, objective, and dramatic; there are three persons and two numbers of voice: first-, second-, and third-person speakers, and singular and plural numbers. This table will help us see who is speaking and what they are speaking about":

| | Voice | | |
	Subjective	Objective	Dramatic
Person			
First	I	I, we	I
Second		you, you (pl.)	
Third		he, she, it, they	

"So all these things depend on each other when you're writing dialogue."

"Yes. Take for instance these sentences in a short play I wrote titled 'Barrow Yard,' which I later turned into a short story titled 'The Yeoman's Story'—they're spoken by a tramp: '. . . and yet you know damn well there ain't a friggin' thing we could've done. He saw our fire, and *bing!* there he was, standing in the firelight.' In 'The Yeoman's Story' the tramp becomes Duke, who is a better-educated person with a middle-class background. The equivalent sentences read, '"You know damn well there's not a thing we could've done about it," Duke said. "He saw our fire, and then there he was, standing in the light."'"

"Aren't we talking about characterization again? How dialogue characterizes the person speaking?"

"That's very largely what diction is about—identifying the persona and his or her traits, including the main personality trait on which much of the story will depend for its plot and the motivations of its characters."

Fred Foyle stands beside the Author with his head turned slightly. He is looking down at a pile of books on the floor. "What are all these for?" he asks. "I saw you bring them in yesterday."

"They're full of examples," the Author replies, his fingers nimble upon the keyboard. "Take this one, for instance." He stops typing to reach down and pick up one of the volumes. "It's a short novel, *Of Mice and Men,* by John Steinbeck. It's about two men, Lennie and George. Lennie is a big man who is retarded. George is his friend, his keeper, in effect, whose purpose in this relationship is to keep Lennie out of trouble. This is some dialogue from early in the story":

Lennie looked timidly over to him. *"George?"*

"Yeah, what ya want?"

"Where we goin', George?"

The little man jerked down the brim of his hat and scowled over at Lennie. *"So you forgot that awready, did you? I gotta tell you again, do I? Jesus Christ, you're a crazy bastard!"*

"I forgot," Lennie said softly. *"I tried not to forget. Honest to God I did, George."*

"O. K.—O. K. I'll tell ya again. I ain't got nothing to do. Might jus' as well spen' all my time tellin' you things and then you forget 'em, and I tell you again."

"Tried and tried," said Lennie, "but it didn't do no good. I remember about the rabbits, George."

"That's more than just characterization," Fred says.

"Okay, then. Analyze the passage for me. What's in it?"

"Well, first," Fred points out, "the relationship between the men is established."

"Which one is dominant?"

"The little man, George. He's in charge."

"What's their station in life?"

"That's easy," Fred says. "Both men are without an education. You can tell that by the base level of diction both use. But you get the impression that George is a good deal smarter than Lennie."

"How so?"

"Lennie can't concentrate. Not only does he *say* he forgets, but his mind wanders even as the two men are talking. Lennie gets hung up on remembering some incident in the past involving rabbits while George is telling him—*again*—where they're supposed to be going."

"Is Lennie crazy, as George states?"

"No, you get the impression that's the wrong word, that George doesn't know the right word—'retarded'—so he uses the approximate synonym, 'crazy.'"

"Where are they?"

"On the road. They're wanderers, bums, probably."

"That's not a P. C. word, Fred. Try 'homeless.' What do you think of the form of the dialogue?"

"You mean the way Steinbeck imitates the diction and syntax the two men use by phonetically spelling their pronunciations of words?"

"That, and the syntax of their sentences."

"I think it takes some getting used to."

"Is it justified?" the Author asks.

Fred Foyle sits on the edge of the La-Z-Boy and puts his chin into his left hand, resting the elbow on his knee. "That's hard to say," he says, finally, looking up.

"Tell you what." The Author turns back to his keyboard and monitor. "Let's take that whole passage and change its level of diction and the syntax of its sentences and see if it makes any difference":

Lennie looked timidly over to him. "George?"

"Yes, what do you want?"

"Where are we going, George?"

The little man jerked down the brim of his hat and scowled over at Lennie. "So you've forgotten that already, have you? I have to tell you again, do I? Good grief, you're a madman!"

"I've forgotten," Lennie said softly. "I tried not to forget. Truly I did, George."

"All right—all right. I'll remind you. I've nothing better to do. I might as well spend all my time explaining things to you so that you can forget them and I can tell you again."

"I've tried and tried," said Lennie, "but it's done little good. I remember what happened to the rabbits, George."

"What a difference!" Fred says. "The whole passage is transformed. They're two other people."

"So Steinbeck was justified in doing what he did with syntax and level of diction?"

"Absolutely."

"Would you try it yourself in a story you wrote?"

Fred looks dubious. "I'm not sure I could pull it off," he says. "While the diction of both Lennie and George is on the same level, for instance, the characters are totally different. I'm not sure I could pull that off," he says again.

Dialect 2

The Author nods. "It's hard. You have to be so confident of your characters and of your level of diction—even of the dialect you're using—that it's easy to let your personas slip out of character."

"What do you recommend, then?"

"Hold on, Fred," the Author says, a fleeting look of annoyance passing over his features. "Let's do this by example. Do you remember that passage we used earlier on from John O'Hara's short novel *Appointment in Samara*?

Fred thumbs back through the manuscript pages lying in their folder on the open top drawer of the two-drawer wooden file. "Sure. Here it is right here—"

"All I want is one section of it: 'What's the mattah, honey sugah lamb pie, what's the mattah you all?' What's that supposed to be?"

"Southern dialect," Fred says without hesitation.

"Not exactly."

Freed peers more closely at the monitor. "Oh, I see what you mean. It's mock–Southern dialect."

"Do you suppose O'Hara was a Southerner?"

"I doubt it."

"Why?"

"Why would a Southerner make fun of his own dialect?"

"Indeed, why would he?" the Author asks archly. "O'Hara was a Pennsylvanian. But there's another reason a Southerner wouldn't normally use 'Southern dialect.'"

"What's that?" Fred asks.

"Because a Southerner doesn't *hear* his or her own dialect. Only someone from another area of the country actually hears it. If you're from Maine, you speak like a Mainer; if you're from Brooklyn, you speak like a Brooklynite. The only way you're going to be conscious of your dialect is if you can somehow get *outside* your dialect and hear it as an observer would hear it. Here's an example," The Author says, picking up another book, "from *Look Homeward, Angel,* by Thomas Wolfe, a southern writer":

"You little freak—wandering around with your queer dopey face. You're a regular little Pentland—you funny little freak, you. Everybody's laughing at you. Don't you know that? Don't you? We're going to dress you up as a girl, and let you go around like that. You haven't got a drop of Gant blood in you—papa's practically said as much—you're Greeley all over again; you're queer. Pentland queerness sticking out all over you."

Fred Foyle looks startled. "Why, there's nothing at all there to show that it's spoken by a Southerner!"

"Just so. The local PBS station here in town has a slogan: 'The pictures are better in the theater of the mind.' That goes for speech, too: 'The dialogue is better in the theater of the mind.' Everyone—Southerner, Northerner, Westerner, Cajun, Navaho—is going to read those words silently and hear them in his or her own version of 'Southern dialect.'"

Slang 1

"In other words," Fred says, 'You're telling me that a writer ought to leave well enough alone." He pauses to mull that thought over. "In that case, why did Steinbeck give a sort of 'slang' dialect (if I can put it that way) to Lennie and George?"

"Because," the Author says patiently, "bums probably aren't going to be reading his book. People who are literate are going to read it, so both Steinbeck and his readers are looking at the world of the characters in *Of Mice and Men* from the outside, not the inside. They are observers. They are reading a book that is not a product of their own class, or their own region or their own dialect."

"But what if somebody wants to write a whole story in a dialect. Can it be done decently?"

"Steinbeck did it, but I think it's time for another whole story," the Author says.

"One of your own?"

"Yes."

Scot on the Rocks

Forrest MacFarlane, the only Scottish ghost on the planetoid Ergos, was in a fever of excitement. At the initial clamor of his spaceship detection unit—a homemade model he'd tinkered together some years before he'd died—he had levitated upstairs and hurried to the big window in the hall of MacFarlane Manor. Now he stood squinting intently into the stars. He licked his somewhat vaguely defined lips as his eyes darted about trying to single out a light that moved in the night sky.

Across the valley MacFarlane could make out, with his sharp old Celtic eyes, his archenemy and sole neighbor Roger Holmesby standing on the balcony of Holmesby House. The tall figure of the British phantom stood limned in its own excited, ectoplasmic aura. He, too, was gazing upward. Evidently Holmesby felt his ears turning red, for he turned and peered across at the Manor for a moment or so. Then, with a leer (MacFarlane felt certain) Holmesby raised a tenuous fist and shook it at the Scot. MacFarlane snorted and began to search among the stars.

The enmity between MacFarlane and Holmesby dated from the day when, seventy-seven years past, Holmesby had wrecked their explorer-craft on Egos and marooned them hopelessly on this tiny clod in the center of the Milky Way. The wreck had been accidental, but its cause had not—Holmesby liked to drink, even on watch, and sometimes he drank too much. As a matter of fact, if MacFarlane hadn't awakened from his sleep and hauled Holmesby's drunken carcass off the controls just before the ship was about to plummet into Ergos, they might have become wraiths immediately upon their arrival. As it happened, though, the pair had spent years on the planetoid in the corporeal state before natural death had overtaken them both.

Since the day of the disaster MacFarlane had hated the Englishman with all the single-minded concentration a Scotsman can bring to bear upon a fellow son of the glorious Isles. Holmesby was Cockney English through and through but, as the Scot took every opportunity to remind him, a relative latecomer whose bloodline dated certainly no farther back than the Jutes.

At last MacFarlane thought he discerned something moving in the sky. His gaze settled upon a single point of brilliance that seemed a bit redder than most of the others, an iota larger than it had been a few seconds earlier. Was it . . . could he dare hope? "Con it be true?" he murmured in his thick burr. "It is, thonk God! A rocket!" A rocket. "Ofter all these years," MacFarlane sobbed. "Solvation fro' this miserable oxistence!"

It had, indeed, been miserable, for not only had he to put up with Holmesby, he had also to live on Ergos which was very small. Its circumference was a mere twenty-five hundred miles, but its density was rather great, so it had a gravity comparable with that of Earth. Its atmosphere was breathable, it had fertile soil, plenty of water—in short, it was entirely livable. From MacFarlane's viewpoint, however, there was something intolerably wrong with Ergos—it looked a lot like England.

In all the planet there was not a true highland to be seen, not an upland stream nor a glen where MacFarlane could seclude himself and dream of the Auld Land; not a stone, not a blade of grass that looked the least like Scotland. There was nothing but a bunch of blasted moors and this valley with its river that looked like the Wye. MacFarlane could only wait—his ectoplasm turning a pallid gray with yearning—and hope that someday a rocket from home would somehow come to carry his shade away from this heavenly Hell.

In the first years it had not been so bad. There had been the house to build, crops to discover and grow, the countryside to explore. Eventually, though, the novelty of the situation had worn off, and MacFarlane had been left with only the prospect of death as a release from his prison, for when MacFarlane had died he had been horrified to discover a scientific principle—one of many such principles, he often bitterly reflected, as no mortal could possibly divine: a ghost may not travel through a vacuum without dissipating its ectoplasm throughout that vacuum. Since all ectoplasm is sentient, any attempt to levitate to Earth would mean scattering one's mind all over the universe. The task of pulling oneself together under such circumstances, of course, would prove Herculean, if not totally impossible. MacFarlane had therefore abandoned himself to hating Holmesby.

Holmesby had died first. Perhaps if Holmesby hadn't decided to haunt MacFarlane in lieu of something better to do, the Scotsman wouldn't have hated him quite so intensely. At any rate, Forrest would have hated the Englishman quite a bit, for in life Holmesby had been a churlish sort of Cockney oaf, but as a shade he began to affect a monocle and the airs of the English country gentry. Worse, he began to refer to himself as "Colonel" Holmesby. He had, in fact, never been higher in the Space Service than Pilot Second Class, and it had been MacFarlane who was in command of their explorer-craft.

These thoughts raced through Forrest MacFarlane's mind in chaotic fashion as he watched the slowly brightening light in the heavens. At last he tore his eyes away and looked again across the valley towards Holmesbty House—it was just a trifle bigger than MacFarlane Manor. It stood on a hillock that was infinitesimally higher than the Scot's, and it was surrounded by trees that were slightly taller and more imposing than those that encircled its counterpart across the valley.

As MacFarlane stood quietly in the breeze that fluttered like an old rag about the house, a wave of rage welled from some floodgate deep within him and coursed along the paths his blood had once taken. "Curse him!" MacFarlane muttered. "O' course, the black knave will attempt to thwart me in my efforts to escape. But he shallna' do it!" Again he mumbled a bleak epithet beneath his nebulous breath and turned once more to the stars.

But he could not concentrate on the approaching rocket. MacFarlane could think only of how much he wanted to leave. And he had to admit that it was probable Holmesby had an equal desire to leave Ergos, but that wasn't the worst of it—only one of them could go. The reason for this situation lay in another of the scientific principles that govern the behavior of ectoplasm. *(Curse scientific principles,* MacFarlane caught himself thinking as he remembered the words—the fateful words of old Prof. MacDougall, late of Jupiter College, Edinburgh—*"The thing we must all remember about basic principles is that they are so widely applicable.")* Though made of the essence of void, ectoplasm reacts to various stimuli and shows many of the properties of a liquid. In the presence of living flesh, ectoplasm displays a tremendous affinity for other masses of ectoplasm.

Thus, if both Holmesby and MacFarlane attempted to stow away on the approaching space ship, the living human beings aboard would act as catalyst, and the two phantoms would merge to form one ghostly (Mac-Farlane thought, *ghastly!*) entity, a prospect neither of the specters could bear even to think about. MacFarlane shuddered. "'Tis a thing that must never come to pass! I must get aboard th' ship forst! Holmesby will *never* dare to follow. I *must* be the forst aboard," the Scotsman whispered prayerfully.

MacFarlane finally refocused his eyes on the rocket and gave it his entire attention. By this time the pinpoint of flame had become very large. A few ragged clouds frothed across his view now and then, making it difficult for him to determine the direction the ship was taking. After a few more minutes of observation, however, he decided that the rocket was approaching the planet directly rather than obliquely. The captain of the ship had evidently decided that the small size of the planet made reconnaissance orbiting too difficult.

As MacFarlane stood on his balcony making mental calculations regarding the ship's landing point he was suddenly startled by a cough behind him. Turning, he saw Holmesby standing in the hallway.

"Good evening, Forrest," Holmesby said.

Standing close beside one another, the ghosts presented quite a contrast. The Englishman was tall and broad-shouldered, attired in evening dress. His monocle twinkled in the starlight, and his walking stick dangled in a debonair manner from his left arm, but there was something about the set of his chin and those shifting eyes. . . .

On the other hand, Forrest MacFarlane was short and thin. Much smaller than Holmesby, the Scot could nonetheless draw himself up with such dignity when aroused that he would appear to be at least the equal of an Englishman. Add to this fact the flashing blue eyes, the stern set of his mouth, the jaunty tartan kilt, and one had a man who was . . . well, a *man*.

MacFarlane eyed Roger Holmesby coldly for a moment then went back to watching the ship.

"I said, good evening, MacFarlane. Haven't you the common decency to answer a gentleman?"

MacFarlane whirled about, his tartan plaid kaleidoscoping in the starlight. "Aye, I hae . . . for a gentlemon. But nae for ye! Yon ship gies me the long-sought, final nay to all yere gab. So, away wi' ye, and dinna come back."

Holmesby laughed and looked at the sky. Then he cackled again. The rickety old house creaked in the wind. MacFarlane was silhouetted in the soft glow of an intense Milky Way, glaring at Holmesby. The Englishman, a mere shadow of himself, sank deep into the tongues of blackness that curled out of the hallway.

"Then 'tis a fight, Holmesby?"

"If you're foolish enough to fight, it is."

"Then on yere way," MacFarlane roared, though it sounded more like a whisper.

The Englishman turned as though to leave, and MacFarlane looked away from him just as the ship came roaring down into the valley. The Scotsman was too excited to remember that one should never turn one's back on Roger Holmesby.

Captain Emilio DeQuinta took the various test reports as they were handed to him and tabulated their results. Seventy-five minutes of calculation proved conclusively that the planetoid on which they had landed was habitable in every sense of the word. He yawned, stretched, and was about to go to his compartment until morning which, he reckoned, would be in about seven hours.

The crew of the Starship Explorer *Orion,* which formed the laboratories and intergalactic home of one hundred members of the Bureau of Extragalactic Surveys, had been working hard during the nine hours of approach. Now that they had landed on Ergos they could bide their time and explore at leisure. A few hours of rest would be, if not absolutely necessary, at least advisable. Captain DeQuinta took a few steps towards the door when, suddenly, it opened and Briggley, the steward, saluted and handed him a note.

DeQuinta took the paper and read it. His eyes widened. He read it again, then he stuffed it into his pocket and started hurriedly up towards the cabin deck where the observatory was located. As he was passing the Zoological Lab, Doug Douglas the young zoologist, hailed him.

"Where to, Captain?" He smiled. Douglas was medium-sized, lithe, and sandy-headed. His face was broad and red, very smooth except around the eyes where creases of amusement were noticeable. It was imperative that every space ship have at least one of these bright, imperturbably optimistic young men aboard, for obvious reasons.

The Captain paused. He glanced at Douglas and said, "I'm off to inspect a bit of real estate."

"Real estate? Can you wait just a moment, Captain, while I encapsulate an animal that's just died? That is, if you don't mind my tagging along."

"Okay," DeQuinta answered, "but hurry it up."

"Be just a sec, sir." Douglas slipped the body of a white rat into a small plastic container, attached a nozzle on its cover to a vacuum pump, and pressed a button. The pump drew all the air out of the container, a valve snapped shut, and Douglas detached the container. He put the preserved rat on a table and turned to accompany DeQuinta. "I'll label it when I get back," the young man said as he fell into step. "Sure wish we had the facilities to carry out all the mortality tests necessary on our own animals." He had to walk fast to keep up with DeQuinta. "What's all this about real estate?"

"Parnassey up in the observatory says she's discovered a couple of houses sitting on some hills right above us. We're going up to take a look."

"Houses! On an uncharted planet? What kind of houses?"

"You know as much as I do. Here we are." The two men reached the cabin deck and went down the passageway to the observatory. Lois Parnassey was standing, petite and pretty even in coveralls, at the great quartz semidome, looking out over the dimly lighted landscape.

As the men approached she turned and glanced at them. Douglas winked at her. She looked down her nose at him, but she blushed. They joined her at the semidome, and she pointed out the houses to them. "See, there they are," she said, "one on that hill, and the other is across the way. You can just make out their silhouettes against the stars."

Douglas permitted himself one more admiring glance before he turned to look out of the semidome. But when he finally caught sight of Holmesby House and MacFarlane Manor he forgot Lois, hard as that was to do. Even in the uncertain light he could see that the former was a Victorian-style dwelling, and the latter was of the rustic type of structure he had seen in out-of-the-way sections of the Scotland he had visited with his parents when he was a child. He'd never forgotten those homes. It was almost as though their recollection was blood memory.

After several minutes of observation Douglas, with all the enthusiasm he could muster, turned to the Captain. "Sir," he said, "why couldn't I go out and look things over? Parnassey could accompany me, and we'd be quite safe. We'd be within hailing distance."

DeQuinta was about to say no, but he was curious also. He would have liked to go, but regulations prevented it for the moment. He hesitated, then he said, "All right, but be careful. Our detectors have found no traces of large living things or toxic substances in the atmosphere, so it's probably safe. But check with the ship regularly. We'll be standing by."

Douglas saluted and broke away. He beckoned to Lois who was staring at him. "Thank you, sir," he mumbled. He grabbed Lois's hand and began pulling her along behind him. Finally she began to hurry too, and the clatter of their footsteps echoed through the cabin deck as they receded into the center of the ship.

By the time they were ready to leave word had spread and the rest of the crew clustered around them talking excitedly. DeQuinta gave a sign. Someone threw the toggle switch that opened the airlock doors—with the first gust that swept into the ship Holmesby entered, sucked in on the wave of fresh air. No one saw him, and if anyone heard his smug laughter, it went unnoticed in the general babble.

"Now we shall see," Holmesby chortled, his invisible face screwing it-self into the caricature of a grin. He settled himself in the Captain's chair in the pilot house, lit a cigar he had dreamed into pseudo-existence, and relaxed contentedly. The first stage of his homeward journey had com-menced—and the hardest stage at that.

While Holmesby was enjoying his smokeless smoke, Douglas and Par-nassey proceeded across the valley towards the abode of Forrest MacFar-lane, originally of Scotland, late of the planetoid Ergos, and likely to re-main. The grass was lush, the valley was peaceful, and the stars cast a goodly bit of light through a clear sky. The young man and woman spec-ulated on the houses and, finally reaching MacFarlane Manor, they exam-ined the structure carefully, taking samples of the wood and stone from which it was fashioned; gathering specimens of dust, dirt, and even some of the insects that crawled and flew hither and yon. It was not until they opened the warped door and peered into the musty hall that MacFarlane's lurid speech could be heard.

Douglas stared into the interior of the house. Lois started backward—their surprise was complete, for the shipboard instruments had definitely indicated the absence of any but the lower forms of life. The zoologist glanced at his colleague and said, "You stay here. I'll be right back." He started forward.

"Doug . . . !" Lois started to call, but it was too late. Douglas was al-ready inside.

It was in the closet on the right-hand side of the front stairs that he found MacFarlane bound tightly in a heaving mass of cobweb filaments. Douglas didn't even need a flashlight for MacFarlane was glowing a furi-ous crimson as he shouted and struggled to be free, though his shouts were more like the rustling of breezes than shouts.

"Weel, dinna stond there lookin' like the onintelligent gowk ye no doobt be!" soughed the phantom, beside himself. Douglas stepped back-ward, his incredulous eyes reflecting MacFarlane's intense light. "Ond dinna run awa', for I willna do ye harm. Free me, if you will, young mon. . . ." His glow faded to magenta as he looked up at Douglas.

It took a good deal of courage to do what Douglas did then. But, of course, to be a spaceman one must have courage and clean habits. Douglas drew his knife and cut the cobwebs binding the Scottish shade, muttering, as he did so, "What the heck are you?" "I, sor, om a Scots-man!" shouted MacFarlane, leaping free. "I micht odd, I om also a gen-tlemon ghost, marooned here some seventy odd years ago. 'Tis long and long I've waited to see ye, laddie, and forgie me for shoutin' at ye the way I did."

Douglas, seeing that MacFarlane was standing away and evidently meant him no harm, shouted aloud, "It's all right, Lois! I'll be out in a few minutes. Keep a watch out there and don't alarm the ship." Then, still looking at the ghost, he shook his head and said, "How do you do, Mr. MacFarlane. I am Lieutenant Douglas of the Starship Explorer *Orion*."

A spaceman sees some strange things, so he gets used to accepting the unbelievable, and gradually Douglas was coming to realize that the Scotsman was not a figment, that he existed—or at least *had* existed at one time. Soon the young man was learning the why and wherefore of MacFarlane's presence, about the marooning of the two spacemen, and about Holmesby who had, by this time, undoubtedly made good his triumph over the Gaelic shade.

"Yes, lod, I'm sore afraid thot despicable English banshee is now resting securely aboard yere ship. Ond how am I to oust him? I cana tell."

"But," asked Douglas, "Why can't you both embark aboard the *Orion*? You wouldn't take up any room at all, you know." MacFarlane knew that Douglas, as a scientist, would understand about general principles, so he explained the properties and propensities of ectoplasm in the presence of a catalyst. "It does look hopeless, Mac," Doug agreed. By this time he was in complete accord with MacFarlane for, although he was not a native Scot, Doug's sense of fair play and MacFarlane's description of Holmesby and his tactics had biased him. "I wish I could help," he said, "but zoologists don't have much to do with ectoplasm."

MacFarlane heard Doug say "ectoplasm" and "zoologist," and the idea hit him. It was so simple, and so beautiful, that he couldn't make words pass his writhing lips for a moment. "Ah, but wait, lad!" MacFarlane finally croaked, his eyes burning like arc lamps. "Ye say ye're the ship's zoologist? Do you still bottle up the wee dead beasties as we used to do?" Doug nodded. "Hark, perhaps I hae a wee plan."

"Can I let my partner in on it?" Douglas asked. He could hear Lois outdoors making impatient noises.

"Are you all right?" she called.

MacFarlane nodded, reluctantly. "Come ye richt back now," he said.

When finally Lois and Doug emerged from MacFarlane Manor it was with smiles. They said nothing and began walking to the ship. Slowly, not too obviously, Doug put his arm around her to help her over the rough places. MacFarlane was right behind them, and he missed nothing.

Forrest MacFarlane waited outside for a while. He waited until a noise, a horrified scream so high in pitch that only he could hear it, resounded throughout the valley. A moment later he gratefully watched the shade of Roger Holmesby emerge from the lock of the ship like a purple streak, pursued by a long and wavering line of ectoplasmic bodies: the shades of all the white mice, hamsters, and rabbits which had given up their lives courageously for science during the course of the *Orion's* voyage, and which now sought to merge with the insubstantial substance which was Holmesby. For, at MacFarlane's suggestion, Douglas had momentarily opened the vacuum-sealed plastic sarcophagi in which the animals had been placed immediately after their giving up the ghost. Now, they were leaving the ship, hot on Holmesby's streaking trail.

Several days later, when the scientists aboard the Orion had satisfied their curiosity regarding the planet Ergos and had marked it for colonization, the starship blasted off. A jubilant Scottish phantom watched the disembodied fists of Roger Holmesby, vibrating madly from the balcony of Holmesby House, diminish swiftly into the distance.

"Dinna worry, ye grommetable Britisher! Another ship wil be along . . . in a coople o'years." Forrest MacFarlane chuckled and settled himself comfortably into a chair in the observatory. "Ond I hope ye enjoy th' company o' yere new neighbors meantime," he murmured sleepily. The sound of the rocket motors was like a lullaby. MacFarlane of Ergos had nothing to do now but wait.

Dialect 3: Standard American

"Whatta ya know," Fred says, "a science-fiction ghost story! I take it that, among other things, it's supposed to illustrate genre writing. Am I right?"

"That, and some of the dangers and problems associated with writing dialect. It's usually pretty hard to get away with. Generally speaking, it's best to stay away from dialect and go with straight standard American diction."

"*Standard* American?"

"Yes, as distinguished from regional American dialects."

"You mean 'standard' like the dialogue of the young couple in the story, Douglas and Parnassey?"

"And Captain DeQuinta."

"I hate ghost stories," Fred mutters, curling his lip and shoving his forelock back into position with an offhand flip of his fingers.

"Why?"

"They're so . . . ," Fred hunts for the word. "Insubstantial."

"No more than you are," the Author retorts. Fred does not reply. He lets his head and his hair hang down while he sits with his thin elbows on his bare knees—he is wearing shorts and a tee shirt. "Sorry, Fred, that was uncalled-for."

"But I see what you mean about dialogue written in dialect," Fred Foyle says leaning back in his chair.

"Don't you think it works?" the Author asks.

"I guess you get away with it because the story is humorous," Fred replies, "but I don't think you would have in a serious story. I notice you didn't try to do a real British dialect with Holmesby."

"No, you're right. There I just used a slightly elevated level of diction to imply his snootiness."

"Whatever made you attempt such a thing in the first place?" Fred sits back in the La-Z-Boy, sticks the little finger of his left hand into his ear and jiggles it.

"I wrote the first draft of that story when I was a teenager learning how to write—I was in the Navy at the time, taking a correspondence course in fiction writing. I guess I just didn't know any better. I wouldn't have tried it if I'd known a bit more about the hazards of dialect writing."

"I'll bet you'd hate to have a real Scotsman read it, eh?" Fred looks up and grins. "Did you ever publish it?"

"In a literary magazine about fifteen years later." The Author's eyes go out of focus as he thinks back. "It even won a prize."

"No kidding?"

The Author can't tell whether Fred is genuinely impressed or just putting him on.

"Even though 'Scot on the Rocks' is a plot story, and the characterization is a little thin, I think I like the old Scotsman," Fred says.

Diction 4: Stereotyping

"Maybe 'thin' isn't quite the right word," the Author replies, frowning a little. "Stereotyped' is maybe more accurate. As a personality, MacFarlane is perhaps the least stereotyped of the characters in the story, but his language is the *most* stereotyped; that is, *typecast*. He sounds like what most people might think a Scot would sound like. What do you like about him particularly?"

"His feistiness," Fred answers immediately, "and his stubbornness; they helped him out in the end."

"The most important weapon a protagonist has in his or her conflict is character. It's in the performance of deeds that the protagonist's character reveals itself. . . ."

"Deeds and speech," Fred interposes, "but isn't it possible for a writer to do a decent job with dialect?"

"How do you like this?" the Author asks:

"Aha!" sez Brer Fox, sezee, "you'r dar, is you?" sezee. "Well I'm gwineter smoke you out, ef it takes a month. You'er mine dis time," sezee.

Brer Rabbit ain't saying nothing.

"Ain't you comin' down?" sez Brer Fox, sezee.

Brer Rabbit ain't saying nothing.

Then Brer Fox he went out after some wood, he did, and when he came back he heard Brer Rabbit laughing.

"W'at you laughin' at, Brer Rabbit?" sez Brer Fox, sezee.

"Can't tell you, Brer Fox," sez Brer Rabbit, sezee.

"Better tell, Brer Rabbit," sez Brer Fox, sezee.

"'Tain't nuthin' but a box er money somebody done gone an' lef' up here in de chink er de chimbly," sez Brer Rabbit, sezee.

"Don't b'leeve you," sez Brer Fox, sezee.

"Look up en see," sez Brer Rabbit, sezee. And when Brer Fox looked up, Brer Rabbit spit his eyes full of tobacco juice, he did, and Brer Fox he made a break for the branch of the stream. Then Brer Rabbit come down and told the ladies good-by.

"How you git 'im off, Brer Rabbit?" sez Miss Meadows. Sez she.

"Who? Me? Sez Brer Rabbit, sezee. "W'y I just tuck en tole 'im dat

*ef he didn't go 'long home en stop playing his pranks on spectubble folks,
dat I'd tak 'im out and thrash 'im," sezee.*

Fred's eyes are as wide as they can get. His jaw is slack and he is
making little gurgling noises in the back of his throat. Suddenly,
his mouth snaps shut. It's a moment before he can say anything.
"What is *that*?" he manages at last. "Is that O'Hara doing mock-
Southern dialect again?"

"No way," the Author types. "That is Joel Chandler Harris, a
nineteenth-century American fiction writer, doing dialogue for
characters in his *Brer Rabbit* series. They're considered to be
children's classics."

"Where was he from?"

"Harris was a native Georgian," the Author replies.

"I thought you said that only outsiders can truly hear the dialect of their region?"

"That's not Southern dialect, Fred. Figure it out. What is it?"

Silence. Then, "It's 'Negro' dialect, isn't it?"

"No. It's Harris' stereotypical conception of how plantation
blacks spoke in the nineteenth century. Harris was almost as much
an outsider as any other white person. How do you like it?"

Fred shakes his head so vigorously that his hair falls down all
over his face. He shoves it back, gets up, and begins to pace as
much as it's possible to do so in the narrow garret. "That's a classic?
It's *extremely* annoying," he says. "I can't imaging reading a whole
story of that, let alone a whole book. Who's that narrating?"

"Uncle Remus. He's an old plantation black who's supposed to
be relating Negro folklore through his animal characters."

"That 'Sezee' stuff is infuriating," Fred says. His voice is a
growl. He suddenly sits down. "What are you trying to tell me?"

"That what one can 'get away with' depends on a number of
factors, including the historical period in which one writes, the
audience for whom one writes, one's talent, and so on."

"No one could get away with writing like that today?"

"No one."

"But it remains a classic?"

Diction 5: Pidgin

The Author shrugs. He drops Harris' book back onto the pile on the floor behind him and picks up another one. "Try this," he says:

> *I started to get up but Makino, the cook, grabbed my arm and translated, "She not angry. Only she say very dangerous Fumiko-san walk with Americans."*
>
> *"She wasn't walking," I cried. "She was sitting here."*
>
> *"Please!" Makino protested. "I not speak good. Trouble too much."*
>
> *Now Mike started to join the Takarazuka girls but Makino pleaded with him, "Soon you leave Japan, Mike-san. I got to stay. Please, no trouble." He whisked away the dishes from which Fumiko-san had been eating and Mike and I sat glumly staring at our mess of tempura.*

Fred looks thoughtful. "I'm not sure," he says. "That's pidgin English, isn't it?"

"More or less. It's from James Michener's *Sayonara,* published about nine years after the end of the twentieth century's World War Two."

"Perhaps he gets away with that," Fred says. "It's not over-done—more a hint of pidgin, I guess, than true pidgin. Is that right?"

Again the Author shrugs. "Some people might consider even that much dialect to be offensive. Here's how James Norman Hall handles a similar problem in *The Far Lands.* It's a book about Pacific islanders, also published after the Second World War":

> *"Mama Ruau, what would he be like—Uri? As a lover, I mean?"*
>
> *"How should I know?" the old woman muttered, testily.*
>
> *"What would it matter, what he is like?" another girl said. "I wish he would take me, just once. I would like to boast that I'd been loved by the nephew of Puaka!"*
>
> *"I've had him," another girl said. The others protested loudly at this assertion, saying that Uri would not even glance at so homely a creature.*

"He didn't care about my face; it was my body he wanted; anyway it was at night that he took me."

"Why haven't you told us before?" another asked.

"Because I knew you wouldn't believe me. But he did. Truly he did."

"Is that supposed to be pidgin?" Fred asks.

The Author shrugs—it's getting to be a habit. "It doesn't matter, does it? If the reader wants it to be pidgin, then it is; if he or she wants it to be Maori or another Pacific language, then it is. Actually, it's standard English in rather simple syntactical constructions. Rather than use some sort of dialect, Hall lets the syntax suggest an uncomplicated life-style."

"But Michener was showing the way some Japanese, who are somewhat conversant with English, would sound in comparison with Americans speaking a rather colloquial English."

"That's true. Hall had no contrasting levels of diction in that passage. Here's how he and his co-author, Charles Nordhoff, handle a scene from their book *No More Gas,* in which a native Tahitian, Jonas, is speaking with two Europeans, a doctor and a lawyer":

"That's all right with me, Monsieur Dorme," Jonas said, when the attorney had finished. "If you got a pen handy I'll sign right off."

"Your sister, Effie, will have to sign with you," the attorney remarked.

"I'll send down for her." Throwing back the coverlet, Jonas got to his feet with surprising agility. Then, remembering that he was supposed to be ill, he said: "I'm feeling a lot better already, Doctor. Shouldn't wonder if it was the cockfight made me feel so miserable. I didn't see how I was going to tell you about that."

The house shook under his tread as he walked across the veranda. Several children were playing below. "Tané, he called. "Run down to Aunt Effie's house and tell her I want her. Right away!"

"And we must have a witness," Dorme continued. "Is there anyone here who could serve? Your cousin, Ropati, of course, would not do."

"I don't want him to know, anyway," said Jonas. "There's no need to tell the rest of the family about this."

"No difference in dialect," Fred says. "Only a slightly heightened level of diction when the doctor and the lawyer speak."

Speech Defects

"But there's enough of it to differentiate between the characters, especially in the context of the story," the Author points out. "By the way, although in their Pacific Ocean books Nordhoff and Hall don't do dialect, in this book they did have one character, a Tahitian named Chester, who stuttered, and they did attempt to show that on the page. Chester in this passage is in a cab; he's been voyaging about, and he's bringing home a fighting cock":

> You du-du-don't need to kill me," his passenger replied. "Take it easy."
> "Thought you was in a hurry to get home?"
> "I am, but you forget what I got back here."
> The driver immediately slowed down. "I wasn't thinking," he said, blankly. "He ain't hurt, is he?"
> "Hope not; bu-bu-but another jolt like that last one. . . . Stop a minute. I want to have a look."

Fred nods. "I'm not sure the authors should have done that, but they don't do much of it, do they?"

"Not much. But in this case the stuttering is a characterizing trait of the Chester persona."

"And there's more done with the levels of diction in that scene, too. The cab driver's speech is base."

Diction 6: Elevation

"You mentioned 'standard American' English," Fred continues. "Is there such a thing as 'standard British' English?"

The Author frowns into the monitor. "I'm not sure there is," he types. "I just recently finished watching the PBS series, *The*

Story of English, the British isles are so regionalized that sometimes a person from one section can hardly understand the dialect of a person from another section." He shakes his head. "Not only that, but the population is stratified in classes as well, and each person can recognize the caste of another simply by hearing him or her speak—think of Eliza Doolittle and Prof. Henry Higgins in the Lerner and Loewe musical *My Fair Lady.*"

"Oh, yes!" Fred says. "I was playing some of your tapes and cd's while you were sleeping the other evening, and I listened to it." He grins and blinks behind the lock of hair fallen across his eyes. "Higgins transforms Eliza."

"Yes, she begins as a cockney who habitually drops initial aitches and calls the professor 'Enry 'Iggins, and ends as a young woman who can't be distinguished from a member of the aristocracy.

"By the way," he says, "that piece of literature began as a drama, *Pygmalion,* by the Irish playwright George Bernard Shaw, was turned into a musical script by the two Americans, and wound up as a screenplay. We'll talk more about that kind of transmogrification in the next chapter."

"*Transmogrification?*"

"Oh, go look it up."

"Okay, I will," Fred says, "but answer my question."

Format and Punctuation 4

"Well, here's a bit of dialogue by the contemporary British fiction writer Frederic Raphael. It's from a story titled 'Sleeps Six.' Something else the British have that differs from us—in addition to a common language—is their use of quotation marks. You'll notice that they start off with single quotes rather than doubles, as we do":

'Oh for God's sake, Philip, pull yourself together. You're behaving like a silly old woman throwing crockery at the wall.'
'If I'm a silly old woman then I'm a silly old woman.'

'You're a silly old woman who's ruining my bloody holiday. I don't mind for myself, I mind for Sherry. I mind for the kids. Pull yourself together.'

'I've had my fill of that. I now propose to pull myself apart.'

Diction 7: Vocabulary and Idiom

"It doesn't look any different to me as far as the syntax of the sentences goes," Fred says peering over the Author's shoulder at the monitor. "But somehow it *sounds* different."

"It's the vocabulary and idiom, mainly, rather than the grammatical constructions."

Fred steps back. "I know what 'vocabulary' means, and I've heard and seen the term 'idiom,' but I've never really gotten a handle on it, if you dig me."

"*Idiom* means, according to the *Random House Dictionary,* 'an expression whose meaning cannot be derived from its constituent elements, as *kick the bucket* in the sense of "to die."' Or, for that matter, *to dig* or *get a handle on* in the sense of 'to understand.'"

Slang 2

"You mean slang," Fred says.

"Not necessarily. An expression may begin as the slang—or 'popular jargon'—of a particular generation, but once it enters the language permanently it becomes an idiomatic expression."

Fred looks at the monitor again. "Scroll back to that speech," he asks, "I'd like to see something—there it is, 'bloody'—that's what you mean by vocabulary and idiom."

"Yes. That term is peculiarly British. They use it nearly all the time, the same way that Canadians are always saying, 'eh?' and Americans say, 'okay'—though in the twenty-first century most of the rest of the world seems to have adopted that particular word as well. And Americans wouldn't say, 'throwing crockery,' we'd say 'throwing dishes.'

"That's the first meaning of 'idiom,'" the Author continues, "but the second meaning is really what this chapter is all about: 'a language, dialect, or style of speaking peculiar to a people.' We could go on forever talking about this, but H. L. Mencken pretty well saturated the subject in his multi-volume *The American Language*. If you want to see the American master of idiom, read Mark Twain, and if you want to see the British master, read Charles Dickens."

"So your use of elevated diction to characterize Holmesby in 'Scot on the Rocks' was unidiomatic, and your use of Scots dialect was stereotypical, and—generally speaking—foolhardy." Fred is clearly enjoying himself.

"*Young* and foolhardy," the Author interjects.

"When, for instance, you have Holmesby say, 'I said, good evening, MacFarlane. Haven't you got the common decency to answer a gentleman?' all you have going for your character is a slightly elevated diction."

Foreign Words and Terms

"*Nolo contendere,*" the Author says.

"Come again?"

"*Nolo contendere*—Latin for, 'I won't argue the point.'"

"Can you do that in fiction?" Fred asks, pointing to the Latin.

"As a matter of fact, it's not a bad idea to stick in, let's say, a bit of obvious French or German, perhaps, to indicate that a character is speaking with an accent, rather than try to imitate the accent. This is from Nordhoff and Hall's *No More Gas* also":

Format and Punctuation 5

"I brought in a three-gallon demijohn of red wine," Chester put in. "It's out in the car. Maybe we could get along without the food till morning."

Eita roa'tu! Fana exclaimed. "We got to have a snack tonight to keep us going. And two more demijohns."

"I take it that foreign words and terms go in italics," Fred observes, "even when they're just being used to give the impression of an accent."

"Always," the Author says. "but let me get back to the question of British English for a moment. I said Dickens was the master of British idiom, but so was Thomas Hardy. Here's a passage from *The Return of the Native,* set in the southwest quarter of England (remember, I'm still using British punctuation, so there's no mistake in the two *single quotes* that begin this dialogue; the second one indicates an *elision,* a missing letter. We'd recognize it if the *'a* were an *'e,* meaning *he*)":

'A faltered on from one day to another, and then we heard he was gone.'

D'ye think he had great pain when 'a died?' said Christian.

'O no: quite different. Nor any pain of mind. He was lucky enough to be God A'mighty's own man.'

'And other folk—d'ye think 'twill be much pain to 'em, Master Fairway?'

'That depends on whether they be afeard.'

'I bain't afeard at all, I thank God!' said Christian strenuously. 'I'm glad I bain't, for then 'twon't pain me. . . . I don't think I be afeard—or if I be I can't help it, and I don't deserve to suffer. I wish I was not afeard at all!"

"That looks hard!" Fred exclaims.

"You have to have confidence you have a total grasp on dialect to try a whole novel of that," the Author says. Fred thinks he hears an edge of envy in the tone of the Author's voice. "Much better just to do what J. R. R. Tolkien, the great British fantasy writer and Medieval scholar, does in his trilogy, *Lord of the Rings.* He just uses elevated diction and a slightly formal syntax to suggest an ancient language":

Gimli shivered. They had brought only one blanket apiece. 'Let us light a fire,' he said. 'I care no longer for the danger. Let the Orcs come thick as summer moths round a candle!'

'If those unhappy hobbits are astray in the woods, it might draw them hither,' said Legolas.

'And it might draw other things, neither Orc nor Hobbit,' said Aragorn. 'We are near to the muntain-marches of the traitor Saruman. Also we are on the very edge of Fangorn, and it is perilous to touch the trees of that wood, it is said.'

"Point taken," Fred says. "Where dialect is concerned, less is more."

"That's the way it is with most things," the Author replies. "Less is always better than too much."

Chapter 4

Types of Speech

"You haven't done much more than mention 'tone' and 'style,'"
Fred Foyle says as he brushes back his foreknot.

Tone and Style 2

"As we're using the terms here, *tone,* according to the *Random
House Dictionary,* is 'a particular expressive quality, way of sounding, or modulation, or intonation of voice'; *style* is 'the mode and
form of expression, as distinguished from the content,'" the Author informs Fred categorically.

"So when you write this—'"I *must* be the forst aboard," the
Scotsman whispered prayerfully'—that adverb, *prayerfully,* is describing the 'tone' of voice in which he is speaking?"

"That's right. However, it's always better for a writer to *show*
tone by context rather than merely describe it."

"How would you do that?"

"Well, I could have done it this way: 'Forrest MacFarlane
clasped his hands and fell to his insubstantial knees. "I *must* be the
forst aboard!" the Scotsman whispered.'"

"Ah!" Fred murmurs. "And how about an example of 'style'?"

Speech 1: Ordinary

"How about several?" the Author asks. "And we'll start with the 'style' of ordinary speech. Let's listen in on a conversation a professor is having with his secretary. Though it's summer and the teacher is on vacation, the secretary has phoned and asked him to come to the office to sign two drop slips, one for an advisee who had to drop a summer school course because she's in the hospital, and one for a student who appeared on the rolls for a short-session summer class but who was mis-registered because she was in fact taking another class."

"That's a lot of exposition," Fred says.

"You'd never understand the conversation without it, believe me," the Author assures him:

"Oh! There 'e is."

"Hel-lo, Ma-ry. Um. Um.

"(Incoherent.)"

"Mmm? Mmm?" (The professor hands her an envelope that was mis-addressed and has been returned by the postal service.)

"I was goin-na look that address up, then I thought . . . (incoherent because the professor breaks in to say),

"Yeah, wouldjyou? . . ." (incoherent because both people are talking at once).

"Yeah, and, uh, when you look it up would, uh (pause) you make a copy of the address for me . . ."

"Yeah."

". . . so I can correct my records?"

"Yeah."

"So, uh . . ." (sound of opening an envelope) ". . . oh, God, there's the bookstore bill."

"Ho ho ho."

"Uh, ayeah, and there's this. . . ."

"I need that. And d'you . . . didjou . . . have any records on this Jennie Jones in your. . . ."

"Never, never laid eyes on 'er."

"Okay, I need your signatures for a drop. She's actually doing an independent study with Frank Bean . . ."

"Ah!"

". . . and it was someone else's error, but she hasta go through all this Mickey Mouse 'cause of it."

(Pause.) "Well . . ."

"The computers will not handle it otherwise."

(Long silence while the professor signes a class drop slip). "Actually, it's the tenth, but I put down the ninth on, ah the. . . ."

"Yeah, Okay."

"Now, whaddo I hafta sign here?"

"Okay, there's two, two places . . . the drop slip. . . ."

"Sign the drop slip. . . ."

"Mmhmm."

"Sign it for what?"

"Advisee . . . you're her advisor."

"Okay. Oyeah, awright."

"Yuh, the Dean agreed and signed it."

"Uhhuh, 'at's right."

"And advisor here."

"Yeah, awwmm, I missed Frank . . . er, y . . . I dunno what I'm thinkin' of, God! Jim Bell this morning, so I think I'm gonnoo sign for him. Give this to her father this weekend, and then she can attach her medical statement and mail it right back to the advisement office. . . ."

"Uh, huh."

"I don't think Jim'll mind 'cuz he said he'd go along with anything, he was agreeable."

"Do we actually talk like that?" Fred asks, bewildered and disgusted.

"No, *you* don't, but the rest of us do."

"It's amazing that anything gets communicated at all! This is one time I'm glad I'm a fictional character."

"An *Irish* fictional character," the Author reminds him. "But people get along because a lot of communication is in context, in knowing each other well, as the secretary and the professor do, and consequently in being one step ahead of each other most times. And there's body language . . . gestures, raised eyebrows, throat clearings, *etcetera, etcetera*—an actor can do some of those things in a play onstage. In this real-life case the professor was looking at papers on the secretary's desk while they were talking."

"Did she know she was being recorded?"

"No."

"Can this conversation be made interesting, or at least coherent?"

Speech 2: Edited

"I don't know," the Author says. "Let's give it a try. We'll have to edit it":

The professor strides down the corridor and turns in at the door marked 39. "Oh! There he is!" the department secretary says, looking up from her desk. She wears glasses and there is an Irish look about her, especially about her smile. Her hair is curly and reddish brown. She sits behind her desk working on several stacks of papers.

"Hello, Mary." The professor walks to the desk and the secretary hands him three forms.

"Thanks for coming in like this," Mary says. "I know it's hot and you're on vacation, but. . . ."

"Not at all," the professor says. "It's a relief to take a break from vacation once in a while." He is dressed quite unprofessionally, in shorts and a tank top. "By the way," he says, "I just pulled this misaddressed envelope out of my mailbox. Can you look up the right address and type a new envelope?" It is extremely hot and humid in the office. A tall floor fan whirls the air about, to little effect.

"O, sure," Mary replies. "I was going to look that address up when it came back, then I thought, 'Maybe he'd like to see that the address has been changed,' so I stuck it in your box instead."

"Would you go ahead and do that? And when you do, would you make a copy of the address for me so I can correct my records?"

"Surely." The secretary takes the envelope and, using a letter opener, slices the top open.

"Before I sign these drops," the professor says, "let me see what's in this other envelope . . . oh, God, it's the bookstore bill!"

"Ho ho ho." Mary gives him a commiserating look.

"You think that's funny, eh?"

"Not really. By the way," she asks, noticing which of the forms he is looking at, "did you have any records at all on this Jennie Jones? She was mis-enrolled in her summer pre-session class."

"I never heard of her." The professor takes out his handkerchief and uses it to wipe the perspiration from his forehead.

"Okay, but I need your signature for a drop anyway. She's actually doing an independent study with Frank Bean."

"Ah!"

"It was someone else's error, but she has to go through all this Mickey Mouse red tape because of it. The computers will not handle it otherwise." Mary shakes her head in pity . . . for Ms. Jones, or the professor, or herself . . . perhaps all three.

"Oops! It's July tenth," the professor says, staring at the form he has just signed, "but I put down the ninth."

"No matter," Mary says. "They won't get it until day after tomorrow anyway."

"Now, what do I have to sign on these other two forms?"

"First, the drop slip. . . ."

"Sign the drop slip as what?"

"You're her advisor."

"Right."

"The Dean agreed and signed it already," Mary points out with a pencil.

"Oh, yes. I see."

"And where it says 'advisor' on this other form" she continues. "I have to get Mr. Bell's signature, too, but I missed him this morning, so I think I'll sign the form for him, and give it to her father this weekend. Then she can attach her medical statement and mail it right back to the advisement office. I don't think Mr. Bell will mind because he said he'd go along with whatever needs to be done."

"Sounds okay to me," the professor says. He signs the last form and straightens up. He lays the pencil down on Mary's desk and turns to go.

"That's better," Fred says, "but it's still boring."

Nonconversations 2: Exposition

"Because there's no dramatic tension in it. There's no story being told; there's no conflict, not even a protagonist, and I'm sticking exposition into the dialogue, which is *not* a good thing to do in modern stories, although in early fiction it was a common practice."

"Got an example of that?"

The Author turns away from the keyboard and reaches into the pile of books on the floor behind him. "Here's a passage from an eighteenth-century short novel, *Rasselas, Prince of Abyssinia* by the British writer and lexicographer Samuel Johnson":

"Sir," said Imlac, "my history will not be long: the life that is devoted to knowledge passes silently away, and is very little diversified by events. To talk in public, to think in solitude, to read and to hear, to enquire, and answer enquiries, is the business of a scholar. He wanders about the world without pomp or terror, and is neither known nor valued but by men like himself.

"I was born in the kingdom of Goiama, at no great distance from the fountain of the Nile. My father was a wealthy merchant, who traded between the inland countries of Africa and the ports of the Red Sea. He was honest, frugal, and diligent, but of mean sentiments and narrow comprehension. . . ."

"They actually *read* stuff like that?" Fred asks.

"Styles and conventions change."

Tone and Style 3: Verisimilitude

"Let's get back to the edited real speech on the floor it's at least the *sort* of dialogue you'd find in a story, isn't it?"

"Some stories."

"Is there a term for the technique you used when you edited the transcription of ordinary speech?"

"It's called *verisimilitude*."

"Good grief! Not another one of those foreign terms! What does it mean?"

"It's Latinate, Fred, but not Latin. It's still English, and it means 'lifelike'—accent on the *like*. Its intent is to give the *impression* of real speech."

Tone and Style 4: Realism

"It's not called 'realism'?"

"No. Realism was a specific literary program—the idea was to write about ordinary people in ordinary situations, using ordinary language, rather than idealized or noble people, using literary language. People like the French writer Gustave Flaubert, the Russian Fyodor Dostoevsky, and the American Stephen Crane, all of them nineteenth-century authors, were realists. In the twentieth century realism turned into a bleaker program, naturalism, which maintained that people's lives were controlled by outside forces, such as economics or environment, or by people's inner limitations. Writers such as the Americans Frank Norris and James T. Farrell wrote fiction that was narrated from a particularly bleak, deterministic viewpoint.

"Verisimilitude was a style that was used by both the realists and the naturalists. Here's a passage from *The Awakening* by the nineteenth-century American realist novelist Kate Chopin; compare it with the Johnson passage above—the setting is the Creole bayou country of Louisiana":

Mrs. Pontellier liked to sit and gaze at her fair companion as she might look upon a faultless Madonna.

"Could any one fathom the cruelty beneath that fair exterior?" murmured Robert. "She knew that I adored her once, and she let me adore her. It was 'Robert, come; go; stand up; sit down; do this; do that; see if the baby sleeps; my thimble, please, that I left God knows where. Come and read Daudet to me while I sew.'"

"Par example! I never had to ask. You were always there under my feet, like a troublesome cat."

"You mean like an adoring dog. And just as soon as Ratignolle appeared on the scene, then it was like a dog. 'Passez! Adieu! Allez vous-en!"

"Perhaps I feared to make Alphonse jealous," she interjoined, with excessive naïveté. That made them all laugh. The right hand jealous of the left! The heart jealous of the soul! But for that matter, the Creole husband is never jealous; with him the gangrene passion is one which has become dwarfed by disuse.

"What a difference in style a hundred years makes!" Fred says leaning forward, elbows on his knees—he is on the La-Z-Boy again. "That doesn't sound anything at all like Johnson. What's going on in fiction these days?"

Tone and Style 5: Minimalism

"Well, at the end of the twentieth century and the beginning of the twenty-first there was a return to a form of realism in literary fiction called 'minimalism.' As Charles Newman put it in an article, 'What's Left Out of Literature' in *The New York Times Book Review* for Sunday, July 12, 1987, 'The presumption seems to be that America is a vast fibrous desert in which a few laconic weeds nevertheless manage to sprout in the cracks.'"

"Sounds sort of the way I feel," Fred says. "Does that apply to dialogue too?"

"Famous Irish nun, Fred."

"What?"

"Abbess O'Lutely! Newman says, 'In minimal fiction, there has never been such a conscious and largely successful attempt to capture in dialogue the elisions and inadvertent rhythms of everyday colloquial speech. . . . ' He gives as an example a passage from Bret Easton Ellis's first novel, *Less Than Zero*":

I drive to Trent's house, but Trent isn't there so I sit in his room and put a movie in the Betamax and call Blair and ask her if she wants to do something tonight, go to a club or see a movie and she says she would and I start to draw on a piece of paper that's next to the phone, recopying phone numbers on it.

"Julian wants to see you," Blair tells me.

"Yeah, I heard. Did he say what for?"

"I don't know what he wants to see you about. He just said he has to talk to you."

"Do you have his number?" I ask.

"No."

"That *is* pretty flat. It sounds sort of like your edited real speech—how does it differ? Can you apply minimalist style to the transcription of the professor's conversation with the secretary?"

"Sure. It would go like this":

The professor, dressed in shorts and a tank top, walks down the corridor and turns in at the door marked 39. "There you are," the department secretary says, looking up from her desk.

"Hello, Mary."

"Thanks for coming in like this." "It's hot and you're on vacation. . . ."

"It's okay. "Oh, I just pulled this misaddressed envelope out of my mailbox. How about looking up the right address and typing a new one?"

"Sure. I was going to look that address up, then I thought. . . ."

"Would you go ahead and do that? And when you do, make a copy of the address for me, okay?"

"Sure."

"Before I sign these drops, let me see what's in this other envelope . . . crap. The bookstore bill!"

"Ho ho ho."

"You think that's funny?"

"Did you have any records at all on this Jennie Jones? She was misenrolled."

"I never laid eyes on her."

"Okay, I need your signature for a drop. She's actually doing an independent study with Frank Bean."

"Ah!"

"It was someone else's error, but she has to go through all this Mickey Mouse because of it. The computers won't handle it otherwise."

"Nuts! It's July tenth, but I put down the ninth."

"No matter."

"Now, what do I have to sign on these other two forms?"

"First, the drop slip. . . ."

"Sign the drop slip as what?"

"You're her advisor."

"Right."

"The Dean agreed and signed it."

"Uhhuh."

"And where it says 'advisor' on this other form" she continues. "I have to get Mr. Bell's signature, too, but I missed him this morning, so I think I'll sign the form for him, and give it to her father this weekend. Then she can attach her medical statement and mail it right back to the advisement office. I don't think Mr. Bell will mind because he said he'd go along with whatever needs to be done."

"Sounds okay to me."

"That's minimal, all right," Fred says. "Is that what dialogue sounds like in a play?"

"Not usually."

"Why not?"

Tone and Style 6: Stage Speech

"Because a play takes place on a stage, not in a book lying in your lap. In the book you can stop, go back, reread a passage to make sure you got it right. But in a play, if you miss something, you've missed it. So dialogue in a play must be extremely clear, emphatic, apprehensible as it swiftly passes—that's going to affect its style, though the tone of a passage is going to be interpreted by the director and the actors, with hints from the playwright's script, of course.

"You noticed all those pauses and gaps in the unedited transcription?"

"How could I miss them?" Fred asks. "There were more of them than words . . . at least it seemed so."

"That's because in real life we do what we do in reading—we pause to think about things, we stall for time, we ask for things to be repeated, we ask our neighbor what we missed . . . or we jump ahead because what we're saying is obvious to the person with whom we are conversing."

"So a play can't imitate ordinary conversation even as well as a story can?"

"But it has to seem ordinary . . . as ordinary as the dialogue in a story or on the street. There has to be a 'willing suspension of disbelief' on the part of an audience when it enters a theatre. The same is true for the reader of a novel or a story. We have to subscribe to a convention . . . in fact, to several conventions."

Tone and Style 7: Stream-of-Consciousness

"Are there other styles besides verisimilitude and minimalism?" Fred asks, still leaning forward with interest.

"Certainly, the last century came up with any number of them, I guess, but a couple of the best known are stream-of-consciousness and surrealism."

"What's that first one about?"

Forms of Dialogue 4: Interior Monologue

"Well, the idea there is to have interior monologues in fiction be reasonable facsimiles of the way the mind actually works. We don't ordinarily think in nice, straightforward sentences—you saw that we don't even talk that way—but we wander off the subject, drop hints to ourselves, do fuzzy things with our syntax, elide. . . ."

"What's that?"

"Leave things out."

"That's interior monologues. But can the same thing be done with dialogue?"

"William Faulkner tried it in his novel *The Sound and the Fury,*" the Author points out "—here's a passage":

its late you go on home
what
you go on home its late
all right
her clothes rustled I didn't move they stopped rustling
are you going in like I told you
I didn't hear anything
Caddy
yes I will if you want me to I will
I sat up she was sitting on the ground her hands clasped about her knee
go on to the house like I told you
yes I'll do anything you want me to anything yes
she didn't even look at me I caught her shoulder and shook her hard
you shut up
I shook her
you shut up you shut up
yes
she lifted her face then I was she wasnt even looking at me at all I could see that white rim
get up
I pulled her she was limp I lifted her to her feet

go on now
was Benjy still crying when you left
go on

"That's even more minimal than minimalism," Fred says, his mouth agape.

"How do you do that?" the Author asks.

"I'm not doing it, you're writing it," Fred replies. "In fiction all things are possible."

"No," the Author shakes his head. "In real life, perhaps, all things are possible, but fiction must be truer to life than life."

"Is that a conundrum?"

Format and Punctuation 6

"No, it's a paradox. That's essentially what we're talking about here. For instance, the person who's thinking those thoughts and saying those things is a retarded person in Faulkner's novel, and the dialogue and narration are supposed to mirror his mind and perceptions. But of course, in real life a severely retarded person wouldn't be able to narrate in fiction at all, so Faulkner uses no punctuation and no capitals (except for Caddy's name and 'I,' for some reason) to give the impression of an illiterate person."

"What would the professor's conversation with the secretary look like treated that way?"

"Let's check it out," the Author suggests:

hello mary
thanks for coming in like this its hot you're on vacation
its okay by the way I just pulled this wrong envelope out can you look up the right address and type a new envelope
hot and sticky in the office big floor fan whirls around
o sure
go ahead make a copy of the address for me too
okay

lemme see what's in this other envelope o god it's the bookstore bill
ho ho ho
you think that's funny
not really

"That's enough of that!" Fred interjects.

"I've never been able to finish reading that Faulkner novel myself," the Author admits, shamefaced.

Tone and Style 8: Surrealism

"Interesting effect, that," Fred says. "What's surrealism?"

"Distortion of reality."

"You mean that Faulkner stuff wasn't distorted?"

"Not in the same way. We might be able to understand that subnormal mind, but surrealism is what they might have called in the 1960's, 'psychedelic'—mind-bending."

"Any writers you can name who used surrealism in fiction?"

"The most famous is probably Franz Kafka, an Austrian who wrote in German. However, in looking over Kafka's work (translated into English, of course), I don't find examples of what I'd call 'surrealist dialogue'—the conversation is more or less 'normal'; it's the situations that are abnormal: Gregor Samsa turns into a huge beetle in 'Metamorphosis,' yet the people continue to speak realistically. The same appears to be true in the work of the Spanish surrealist playwright Federico Garcia Lorca. In the surrealist fantasies of the Colombian novelist Gabriel Garcia Marquez there's not much dialogue at all. If you'd like, though, we can try treating the professor's conversation with the secretary surrealistically":

The professor, dressed in shorts and a tank top, walks down the corridor and turns in at the door marked 39. "There you are," Mary says, looking out from under her desk.

"Hello, Mary. How's your picnic going?"

"*Thanks for coming in like this.*" The professor notices that Mary is a green frog today. "*It's hot and you're on vacation,*" she croaks. She is eating a beetle sandwich. Gregor Samsa tries to call for help but his mouth is full of mayonnaise. He's afraid he's going to croak soon himself.

"*It's okay. Oh, I just pulled this misaddressed codfish out of my lobster trap. How about looking up the right address and hooking a new one for me?*"

"*Sure. I was going to look that address up, then I thought. . . .*"

"*Thought is an exercise in anguish,*" the professor says, joining Mary under her desk. "*May I have a bit of that?*"

"*Help yourself,*" Mary says handing him the hoagie roll.

Gregor looks angrily out from between slices of bread at the professor who takes a gingerly bite. "*Would you go ahead and do that, then? And when you do, make a copy of the address for me, okay?*" Gregor has begun to fight back.

"*Sure.*"

"*Before I sign those, let me see what's in this other envelope . . . oh, no. A Venus flytrap.*"

"*Ho ho ho.*"

"*You think that's funny?*"

"*Not really,*" Mary says. "*It's just my sister-in-law. I was wondering when she was getting back from vacation. By the way, did you have any records on this Jennie Jones? She was misanthroped.*"

"*I never laid a tentacle on her.*"

"You want to give me a break?" Fred asks. "That's just ridiculous. It's nonsense, not surrealism."

"Well, you wanted to know. Now we both know why there's not a lot of unusual dialogue in surrealist fiction, or drama either, for that matter. The distortion of reality is in the situation, primarily, though there is a formula for turning an ordinary sentence into a surrealistic one that might work with dialogue as well."

"What's that?" Fred asks.

"Exchange the subject of a sentence for the object. For instance, 'I gave the gorilla a large banana' would become, 'I gave the banana a large gorilla'; or, 'Look! The meat is eating the lion!'"

His head shakes Fred with distaste, causing his eyes to fall down over his hair. "That doesn't appear to be a very promising technique," he says, "either in a play or a story. By the way, did I understand you to say that a play can't imitate ordinary conversation even as well as a story can?"

Literary Conventions

"No. I meant to say that in both fiction and in drama dialogue has to *seem* ordinary . . . as ordinary as the dialogue heard on the street, but it has to be clearer than in a story, more emphatic, and there has to be a 'willing suspension of disbelief' on the part of an audience when it enters a theatre. The same is true for the reader of a novel or a story. We have to subscribe to a convention . . . in fact, to several conventions."

"Name some," Fred says.

"Well, we have to begin with drama, then, because, as we noted in the introduction, the oldest form of fiction is the epic poem, and the second oldest is drama. The oldest form of drama that we know about in the Western world is classical tragedy. Aristotle was the first critic to study the extant plays and to distill from them certain conventions that had already been developed by the playwrights, but never before codified."

Fred looks puzzled. "What's that mean?"

"Written down in an orderly fashion. The first of these had to do with the ability of the audience to suspend the knowledge that they were sitting in a theatre rather than experiencing vicariously what was happening on the 'stage.' Aristotle noticed that most plays exhibited what he identified as the three 'unities' of time, place and action.

"The 'unity of time' is more evident in the theatre than on the page. Members of the audience are seated in a hall and they always know, at least unconsciously, that they are spending several hours looking at a play. If we ask them to believe that during two or three hours of theatre time, a lifetime of stage time is passing, they will tend to disbelieve the relative possibility. But if they are asked to believe that during two or three hours of theatre time a single day of stage time elapses—twenty-four hours, the relative time lapse is much more believable, and this is the reason for the convention, in tragedy, of the unity of time."

"You know, that actually makes sense." Fred nods his head firmly. "How about the unity of place?"

"It's physically difficult to keep changing scenes on stage to indicate different settings. In modern times this difficulty has been overcome to a degree, but in antiquity plays were enacted in open-air amphitheatres. There were no overhead flies for the storage of backdrops, no projectors for throwing films or slides on a screen. Thus, a willing suspension of disbelief was more likely to take place if the audience were asked to believe that the action took place in a single setting—which led to Aristotle's isolation of the convention of the unity of place."

"All right!" Fred says. "Let's have the unity of action now."

"Aristotle noticed that every action in tragedy has a beginning, a middle, and an end, each of proper proportion—neither too large to be seen whole, nor too small to be seen clearly."

"And that's it?" Fred asks. "It's that simple?"

"That's it."

"What's your point—that the rules hold for fiction as well as drama?"

"Well, those rules haven't 'held' throughout the centuries, but they're good 'rules of thumb'—touchstones, as it were. There's been a lot of changes in entertainment and the mass media over the centuries, particularly physical and technological changes. New forms of drama and storytelling have been invented—audio forms of various types including radio and recordings; audio-visual forms as well—cinema and television, for instance. There have even been several revolutions in recent centuries in the print media; during the last quarter of the twentieth century the changes were both numerous and spectacular, as, for instance, the internet."

"You keep making the connection between drama and dialogue in fiction," Fred says, sounding a bit like Nan Deditter, "but is there some real relevance here, or is it just a mania of yours?"

"Before I answer that question," the Author remarks, turning again to lean past the hovering Foyle for a book on the floor, "let me just quote you this passage of dialogue from Arthur C. Clarke's novel, *2001: A Space Odyssey*. Hal, remember, is a computer":

"This is Betty. Start pumping sequence."

"Pumping sequence started," repeated Hal. At once, Poole could hear the throbbing of the pumps as precious air was sucked out of the lock chamber. Presently, the thin metal of the pod's external shell made crinkling, crackling noises, then, after about five minutes, Hal reported:

"Pumping sequence concluded."

Poole made a final check of his tiny instrument panel. Everything was perfectly normal.

"Open the outer door," he ordered.

"That's a great novel!" Fred breathes. He sits back in the La-Z-Boy.
"No, it isn't."
Fred jerks forward. "What are you talking about? Sure it is!"

Novelizing

"It's a great movie, remember?"

Fred says nothing. At last—"What's your point?"

"I have a friend, the Scottish novelist Campbell Black, who novelizes screenplays under a pseudonym or two or three. There's lots of money in it."

Dollar signs click on in Fred's eyes. The Author continues, "It says on the jacket of this book, 'A Novel by Arthur C. Clarke, Based on a Screenplay by Stanley Kubrick and Arthur C. Clarke.'"

Fred nods. "So it started out as a play, a filmscript. That's what you were hinting at when you talked about *My Fair Lady* a while back, isn't it? But doesn't the route usually go the other way? I mean," Fred clears his throat, "don't stories usually get turned into screenplays or dramas or whatever?"

The Author shrugs. "Sure, but it doesn't have to—all roads run two ways. Why don't we check fiction-to-screenplay first, though? Here's a bit of chapter two of John Steinbeck's *The Grapes of Wrath*. A truckdriver has just finished eating":

In the restaurant the truck driver paid his bill and put his two nickels' change in a slot machine. The whirling cylinders gave him no score. "They fix 'em so you can't win nothing," he said to the waitress.

And she replied, "Guy took the jackpot not two hours ago. Three-eighty he got. How soon you gonna be back by?"

He held the screen door a little open. "Week-ten days," he said. "Got to make a run to Tulsa, an' I never get back soon as I think."

She said crossly, "Don't let the flies in. Either go out or come in."

"So long," he said, and pushed his way out. The screen door banged behind him. . . "Well, don't do nothing you don't want me to hear about." The waitress was turned toward a mirror on the back wall. She grunted a reply. . . .

The hitch-hiker stood up and looked across through the windows. "Could ya give me a lift, mister?"

"The driver looked quickly back at the restaurant for a second. "Didn't you see the No Riders sticker on the win'shield?"

"Sure—I seen it. But sometimes a guy'll be a good guy even if some rich bastard makes him carry a sticker.

"And here's the same scene which begins the screenplay by Nunnally Johnson":

Waitress. *When you be back?*
Driver. *Couple a weeks. Don't do nothin' you wouldn't want me to hear about!*

We see him climbing into the cab of the truck from the right side. Getting behind the wheel, he is releasing the handbrake when Tom appears at the driver's seat window.

Tom. *How about a lift, mister?*
Driver. *Can't you see that sticker?*

He indicates a "No Riders" sticker on the windshield.

Tom. *Sure I see it. But a good guy don't pay no attention to what some heel makes him stick on his truck.*

"That's pretty close," Fred says.

"Remember, though, that Johnson has already cut out the whole first chapter of Steinbeck's book. The screenplay is going to be a considerably compressed version of the novel. But there's no reason in the world why a story written entirely in dialogue can't be told using the techniques of fiction, and it's done often these days. Generally speaking, the process is going to be reversed—drama is going to have to be expanded when it's turned into fiction."

"Any examples?"

Nonconversations 3: Silence in Dialogue

"Sure. Here's a short experimental play that, though it's set up as a dialogue, is really a monologue plus silence."

"What?"

"You heard me," the Author says. "What's more, it's a poem written in decasyllabics."

"Deca-whats?" Fred asks, arching his brows.

"Ten-syllable lines. We have two characters, one named Pocoangelini and the other named Mr. Earth. The scene is a beach or some other sandy spot. It's night, and Mr. Earth is making like an ostrich."

"How's that?"

"His head is buried in the sand."

"That's a myth," Fred says.

"Not in this play, it's not. Note that, on the page, the spaces between the speeches are going to vary to indicate shorter or longer silences":

Pocoangelini 7

Pocoangelini. *Sir. Your head. It is stuck into the sand.*
Mr. Earth.
Pocoangelini. *I'm not sure I understand. You hear me,*
    don't you, even with both your earholes squat
    up against those furrows? I say, YOUR HEAD
    IS STUCK IN A BRAIN'S HARROWING. There's dirt
    up your nose and ants are crawling about
    your neck. YOUR HEAD'S STUCK IN THE FILTHY SAND!
Mr. Earth.

Pocoangelini. *The moon is out. It's playing with your spine.*
    the shafts of starfire are sticking in your
    shoulderblades, making you appear to be
    a short of celestial porcupine. What
    are you looking for? What color is the
    inside? Have you found whether stones push each
    other when they are together alone?
Mr. Earth.

Pocoangelini. *Look, I'll scoop you out so we can talk like*
    human beings. It's a cold night. Your thoughts
    must be chilly. This is no hour for such
    silver. I'll dig. Now pull, and tell me. . . .
Mr. Earth.

Pocoangelini.   *Oh!*

"That's as absurd as that ridiculous surrealist dialogue," Fred says.

"Absolutely true," the Author agrees; "in fact, it's called 'theatre of the absurd,' about which you can learn more in our companion volume, *The Book of Literary Terms,* but we won't discuss that topic here. We'll just turn it into fiction":

As he was walking along the moonlit beach Pocoangelini stopped suddenly in amazement. Could it be. . .? Yes, it was! It was somebody kneeling on the shore, his head buried in the sand. Poco walked closer. The moonlight made everything look like quicksilver and ebony. When he reached the figure, Pocoangelini stopped and leaned forward. "Sir," he said politely. "Your head. It is stuck into the sand."

Pocoangelini waited, but all he could hear was the sound of the tide coming in. "I'm not sure I understand," he said. "You hear me, don't you, even with both your earholes squat up against those furrows?" He leaned closer, his hands clasped behind his back. "I say, Your head is stuck in a brain's harrowing. There's dirt up your nose, and ants are crawling about your neck. Your head's stuck in the filthy sand."

Still there was no reply, only the wind rustling the reeds. Pocoangelini cleared his throat. "The moon is out. It's playing with your spine. The shafts of starfire are sticking into your shoulderblades, making you appear to be a sort of celestial porcupine." He paused a moment and straightened up. "What are you looking for? What color is the inside? Have you found whether stones push each other when they are together alone?"

Pocoangelini stood listening for a long while, waiting in the quiet sounds of surf and breeze. The moon scudded overhead like a schooner. At last he too knelt on the beach. "Look, I'll scoop you out so we can talk like human beings," he said. "It's a cold night. Your thoughts must be chilly. This is no hour for such silver. I'll dig. Now pull, and tell me. . . ."

Pocoangelini saw at last that it was Mr. Earth. They knelt gazing into each other's eyes in silence for a long while as the tide came in and the moon sailed toward the west. At last Pocoangelini understood. "Oh!" he said.

That's another *tour de force*," Fred says, "and it's not really a story."

"No, it's an episode."

"Are there any well-known examples of dialogue utilizing silence?"

"How about the opening of Mark Twain's *Tom Sawyer*?"—

"Tom!"

No answer.

"Tom!"

No answer.

"What's gone with that boy, I wonder? You TOM!"

No answer.

The old lady pulled her spectacles down and looked over them about the room; then she put them up and looked out under them. She seldom or never looked through them for so small a thing as a boy; they were her state pair, the pride of her heart, and were built for "style," not service—she could have seen through a pair of stove-lids just as well. She looked perplexed for a moment, and then said, not fiercely, but still loud enough for the furniture to hear:

"Well, I lay if I get hold of you I'll—"

She did not finish, for by this time she was bending down and punching under the bed with the broom, and so she needed breath to punctuate the punches with. She resurrected nothing but the cat.

"I never did see the beat of that boy!"

She went to the open door and stood in it and looked out among the tomato vines and "jimpson" weeds that constituted the garden. No Tom. So she lifted up her voice at an angle calculated for distance and shouted:

"Y-o-u-u Tom!"

There was a slight noise behind her and she turned just in time to seize a small boy by the slack of his roundabout and arrest his flight.

Fred Foyle is silent himself for a moment. Then he breathes deeply and says, "That's just wonderful writing! Even though Tom Sawyer hasn't said anything yet, you now what he's like; you know what his aunt is like, you've got the scene—"

The Author nods, grinning into the monitor. "It was one of the first books I fell in love with when I was a kid. But why don't we turn a short play into a whole story so we can see the process of novelizing worked out completely, even though it's going to be on a small scale? This is a little play I wrote when I was about twenty years old, I guess it was."

Fred looks skeptical.

"Don't say it, Fred," the Author admonishes his fictive friend. "The playlet was called 'Barrow Yard', and it's written in iambic pentameter couplets."

"Like Shakespeare?"

"Well, yes, but not really, Fred."

Barrow Yard

. . . a railroad trestle on the outskirts
of a city; a fire beneath it.
Two hoboes, side by side,
tending a pot of stew
upon the flames. Night:
a trifle misty . . .

Hobo: Hmph! I wonder when that ox will show.
He's slow. And dumb as hell. Y'know,
there's times I wish we hadn't gone and let
him feed with us that night back in. . . .

Tramp: . . . and yet
you know damn well there's not a friggin' thing
we could've done. He saw our fire, and BING!
there he was, standin' in the firelight.
It'll probably be the same damn thing tonight—
he'll stand there sayin' not a single word
till we invite him over. It's sure weird
the way he acts; almost like he was nuts.

Hobo: You have to admit he's got a lot of guts,
   though. Did you see him in that whoppin' fight
   they had down at the Yard? That boy's all right
   when it comes to flingin' fists. I wouldn't want
   to block 'is way when he's out on a jaunt!

> . . . noises in the underbrush,
> rough and fast . . .

Tramp: Ssst! Knock it off. I think I hear 'im comin'.

Hobo: He's makin' lots of noise. Hell! I think he's runnin'"!
   Here he is—!

> . . . the sounds cease:
> a huge man in the glow of
> the fire. A couple of
> heavy strides forward . . .

Hobo (softly): He's makin' straight for you."

> . . . again the great figure
> stops, gazes dully at the Tramp.
> An atmosphere of depression and
> taut silence settles down
> upon the trio. The Tramp
> makes an effort to dispel the
> quietude, divert the gaze
> of the newcomer . . .

Tramp: Hi, Jake. Dig in an' grab a little stew,
   boy. Looks as though you've worked up quite a sweat.
   Do you good to smoke a butt and set
   around for just a while. Been at the Yard?

Jake: Yeah:

Tramp: You see Chuck Walters there? (snicker) He's a card!

Hobo: He's two of 'em—Jack-Ace . . . , y'get it, Jake?

> . . . feigned laughter; not a flicker
> of expression touches Jake's face . . .

Tramp: Seddown, boy. Here, just let me up an' make
a pot of coffee. . . .

Jake: I just killed a man.

> . . . silence again. Moments pass.
> The Hobo makes an attempt at nonchalance . . .

Hobo: Who was it, Jake? You get into a fight,
or something?

Jake: Naw, this here is just my night.

Tramp: Your night for what?

Jake: It's just my night.

Hobo: Watch it!

> . . . Jake leaps, sharp metal in his hand
> showing reflected red from the fire . . .

Hobo: That shiv!

Tramp: I got 'im.

Hobo: Hell!

Tramp: He's hit . . . ,
he's down. My god! I told you once that he
was nutty as a friggin' chestnut tree!
It looks like he's out cold.

Hobo: He's dead.

Tramp: Dead!

Hobo: Y'hit 'im with that board—caved in 'is head.

> . . . a train rumbles over the trestle.
> The wind sharpens between its girders,
> and a few drops of rain fall sizzling
> into the embers of the fire, which has died . . .

Tramp: Hmmph. Dead! Well, let's both head for Barrow Yard.
It's cloudin' over, soon be rainin' hard.

"That's about as minimal a narrative as I can imagine," Fred Foyle says leaning over the printer.

When the last sheet has rolled out of the laser printer Fred picks it up and takes it to his chair with him. "It's nothing but dialogue and a few lines of scene-setting. Is it realism or naturalism?" he asks. The Author doesn't reply—he is absorbed in something he sees on the monitor. "Well, whichever," Fred continues. "It's colloquial diction and base style, and you utilize silences in it. What's going to happen now?"

Transcription and Adaptation

The Author comes to and cocks his head to look over at Fred in the La-Z-Boy. "I promised you a transcription and adaptation to fiction of 'Barrow Yard.'"

"You actually turned that little episode into a story?"

"Yes. It's the second piece in a small trilogy called 'Shipmates,' all three of which are frame narratives—remember that?"

Fred nods. "It's that Joseph Conrad viewpoint from *Heart of Darkness*."

"Right. And the setting here is also aboard a ship, in this case a gun mount on an old carrier, the U.S.S. *Hornet* (CVA 12), circa the mid-1950's, at night. Some sailors are sitting around drinking coffee and telling stories."

"You were quite a copycat when you were young, weren't you?" Fred asks.

"Maybe," the Author replies hunching his shoulders defensively, "but I was really in the Navy then, though I wrote the story version later. If I did imitate, it's not a bad way of learning how to do something—take a model and see how well you can do the same thing. But that's certainly not what I was doing consciously when I adapted this little play. It's the second story in this little trilogy."

Shipmates

The Bo'sun's Story

"The Sea's a big fat heart," says the Bo'sun leaning over the rail of number three gun mount. He leans so largely that in the darkness of the Pacific night his chin seems to drag in the waves like a prow, but the waves are only shadow, and the illumination that casts his face into swells and troughs does not come from roiling plankton, but from a cigarette held loosely in his hand.

Behind him a hatch opens and spreads light over the steel deck underfoot. A radio blares out with the glare—in the gun shack seven sailors lie and sit, listening to some sloe-eyed siren who sings that she don't want no yo-yo, so it sounds; or pouring coffee into the big regulation cups liberated from the galley; or mulling over two of a kind against a possibly full house. The hatch swings to again, and the night closes once more around the mount.

"It was in them Oklahoma nights that I heard her pounding first," the Bo'sun says. "I guess you'll say I'm nuts to hear the sea beating under a lot of red clay. But that's the way it was. I can even remember the first night I figured out what it was there off in the distance, just whispering like, at the edges.

"I'd went upstairs early that night when my pa come home drunk. We owned a farm, or the bank did. It was the first day of the month, and ma and me knew he'd come home smashed into a buzzard's tail. He always did the day the bank payment was due. In the morning of such a day we'd all rise hard out of our beds and drag downstairs. Everything was a coat of dust. You got so you didn't notice it usually, but on these days the dust would sift in with the moonlight, I guess, through sashes and panes, and in your nose it would make a smell like rust that you couldn't wash down even with a cup of mucky coffee.

"We would rise up and go down to sit at the table, quiet, while ma made the breakfast. She would serve it, and pa wouldn't say nothing, just sit there squint-eyed and hard, thinking about the money.

"You don't raise much on a little Oklahoma farm, no matter how hard you scratch. It wasn't pa's fault, you just don't raise much. And the bank don't know nothing about wheat or corn or swine or drought, or the red dust and the wind.

"That wind. It never stopped, or almost never. In the morning it would blow from the east. Sometimes it was strong enough to lean against, and you could see the landscape blowing over from miles gone. At noon it would quit for a breather, just long enough for the sun to bake the land flat into its fields and ruts. Then it would start all over, from the west, and the countryside would blow past again, back where it came from. That dirt could never settle long enough to grow anything. Even when it got wet with a good rain all you had was a foot of mud, hardpan underneath, and the mud would run off into the creeks until you got a drought and the creeks dried up. Then the wind would blow it all back up again. You can't grow nothing but weary on land like that.

"After breakfast pa would take out his wallet and begin pulling greenbacks out of it. He'd take them out one by one and slap them down flat hard on the table. He'd look at each one before he pulled out another. Nobody would say a word. When he was done counting he'd gather them all back up, get up, stuff them in his pocket, and put his wallet back away. 'I'm goin' into town,' he'd say then, and he would leave.

"Once he was gone I'd go do the chores and ma would fix up the kitchen and the rest of the house.

"He'd be gone all day. I would have some time to myself if it wasn't a school day, so I'd spend my time out in the fields or the brush woods. I remember I had a pet horn-toad named Sam. I would gather him up and put him in my shirt pocket head down. He'd stay there that way or, if I put him in tail first, he'd look around a while and then get out and crawl around on my shoulders. I fed him flies from the barn, or put a string leash on him and let him forage on his own. I did other things to kill time, I guess, but that's the thing I remember best.

"The day would be over some time, though, and I'd make my excuses to get to bed before pa got home. My ma would nod as she sat by the kitchen stove darning or something, and it was then that I felt sorriest, for I knew she'd have to wait up till he got home, and he'd beat the shit out of her. He never did that any time but the one night a month, but I hated his pus gut for that. It wasn't for years that I figured out why she'd wait like that, just rocking and darning, till he cracked open the door and smashed her across the face with his open hand. She was a little woman, but not sickly little. She'd wait, and when he'd come in she'd look up at him scared some, but a funny glint in her eyes.

" 'You done this to me,' he'd say, the night wind blowing in 'round him, making the kerosene stove flicker and smoke. 'You've bought my spirit for a pound of flesh and crucified my heart with a son. You've got this coming, you and womankind.' And he'd hit her till she laid crying on the linoleum tiles. The smell of liquor would cloud the room. And then he'd lift her and take her off to bed where he'd pound her belly against the sheets, and her cries would be different, but just as fearful. Or worse. Because now you could hear the pleasure in them.

"Then the house would settle down into the red dark, and the plains and fields would begin to whisper to the walls. In my bed my toad would settle into my side, but I would listen for the sounds of the dust riding moonlight sliding through the windows. Out of the stars the wind would begin to come up stronger—you'd know what it felt like if you tried, to be a limb of a tree creaking in the night.

"But under it all there was a strange sound, like wet things sliding over each other, and strange animals walking on the bottom of things. First far off, making a roar just under your eyelid, then slimming off, then a roar again—if you didn't listen you didn't know it was there, not with your whole mind. And a smell, a smell from way back and way down deep. And then one night I remembered that it was the sea, and I'd never rest until I saw it. Then sleep took me with my eyes stark open, and I heard my mother sigh once from her dark covers before I dropped off the quiet edge."

The Yeoman's Story

"I ran away from home when I was sixteen," Yeoman Fairall said when the Bo'sun had finished talking. It was hard to see in the dark, but the gun lay in silhouette against the stars, and here and there the outline of a sailor lounging on the mount. The ship and the sea made their noises.

"I hadn't been on the road long before I fell in with an old hobo named Duke, a younger one named Corky, and Jake. I don't know how to describe Jake. Duke had some education, but he wouldn't talk much about his past. I had to pry it out of him over a period of time.

"One night he sat looking into the fire and he said to himself for the umpteen-thousandth time, 'It's logical.' He always began by being amazed at his presence in a place like that—an abandoned brickyard on the outskirts of some town somewhere on the prairies, or in the South, or anywhere else. But when he'd asked himself how he'd gotten where he was and had retraced his route from its beginning to a particular campfire, he always ended by saying the same thing: 'it's logical.' Duke was proud of only one thing—that his mind hadn't deteriorated, like about everything else, over the years. He raised his eyes from the fire. In the falling dusk we could see the walls of the old brickworks surrounding us, the caved-in stacks of brick, pretty well raided by the population of the dying town, the faded lettering painted on the side of a broken-down building that formed one side of the place:

BARROW YARD

BRICKS AND

BUILDING MATERIALS

WHOLESALE ONLY

"Duke dropped his eyes to the fire again, and I could see he was letting his mind walk back along that old road. There was the growing up, in good shape, in Illinois—a small city near Chicago just before the war. He had had some ambition then. And there had been the couple of years of college before Pearl Harbor. It looked like he was going someplace in those days—his father's small factory was waiting for him. Elise was waiting for him, too.

"Elise had still been waiting for him when he got back from the Pacific, but there had been no time to finish his degree, because of his father's death in 'forty-four, just before Duke's return. And there'd been the business slump that hit a few marginal industries during the shift to a post-war economy. The plant, engaged in war work for a few years, had put its profits into expansion, and when the fighting ended there was nothing left to pump into another changeover. Duke was under a lot of pressure in those days, and he hadn't been very well prepared to walk out of Guam and the Philippines into Illinois and take on the job of saving the family firm.

"No wonder his marriage hadn't lasted, especially after Elise miscarried their first child. After that it had been a steep slope downhill for Duke—business failure, his mother's broken health and her death grieving over the smash of everything. She'd had only the one son.

"Then the heavy drinking for a few years, and the waking, one morning, to find himself staring into the flames of the first campfire and asking himself how he had gotten where he was. And, of course, the answer.

"Duke nodded. 'It's logical,' he said to himself again. "'what is' Duke looked up to see Corky approaching the fire with a stack of wood. Corky dropped the pile nearby and squatted to warm his hands. 'What's logical?' he asked again.

"Corky was heavy, dressed in jeans and an old leather jacket. Corky's presence was logical too—he was on the run from something, none of us had bothered to ask what. We didn't want to know. Duke lifted a hand to run it over his face, rough with stubble, thin and hollow. He shrugged. 'Us,' he said. "Corky grunted, like he always did. I guess it irritated him when Duke went into his memory routine. 'Not to change the subject,' he said, 'but when's Jake going to show, I wonder? He's been gone a long time. Maybe one of us should've gone with him.'

"Duke shrugged again. 'He'll be back.' 'I sure hope he brings some grub.' Corky liked to talk, but he was quiet for a time, and we watched the fire crackle and cast strange figures into the dusk and the thin mist that was settling on Barrow Yard.

"'I've got a feeling we better not wait,' Corky said finally. 'I got a surprise I been saving.' He got up, went over toward the gate of the Yard, and came back with a paper bag. He squatted and opened it. 'I ran across a truck garden while I was out looking for wood.'

"We looked in and saw vegetables—carrots, cabbages, celery, some small potatoes. 'Not bad,' Duke said. He reached over to his pack and got the pan he always carried, and a box of salt. 'There's a stream near here. I'll get some water and you start on the vegetables.'

"He got up and went through the gate. It was still barely light enough for him to make his way down to the woods, but he had to go carefully. By the time he got back Corky and I had finished paring. Duke arranged the pan in the fire, salted the water, and we threw in the vegetables. We sat awhile smelling the aroma that started to rise from the stew.

Finally Corky broke the quiet. 'Man, that Jake is slow,' he said. 'And dumb. I hope be brings some meat. There's times I wish we hadn't of gone and let him feed with us that night.'

"'You know damn well there's not a thing we could've done about it,' Duke said. 'He saw our fire, and then there he was, standing in the light. Probably be the same thing tonight. He'll stand there saying nothing till we invite him over.' Duke shook his head. 'It's sure strange, the way he acts.'

'Yeah, but you got to admit he's got a lot of guts.' Corky's voice showed his admiration. He stirred the pot. 'Remember the fight in the freight yard when that yard man found us outside Denver? That boy's all right in a pinch.'

"'Knock if off,' Duke said. 'I think I hear him coming.'

"We listened. From the direction of the woods there were noises in the brush, hard and fast. Corky looked up. 'He's sure making a racket.' We listened again. 'Hell,' he said, 'I think he's running.'

"The crackling noises stopped, and we could hear heavy footsteps slowing down, coming across the packed dirt of the yard, but it was too dark by then to see much. Then there was that huge man in the glow of the fire. He took a couple of steps forward.

"Corky said it low—'He's making straight for you, Duke.'

"We saw Jake stop and gaze down at Duke who got to feeling uncomfortable after a while. He cleared his throat. 'Hi, Jake,' he said. I guess something told him not to ask about the meat. 'Dig in and grab a little stew, boy. Looks as though you've worked up quite a sweat. Do you good to smoke a butt and sit down for a while. Where you been?'

"'In town,' Jake said. His voice was thick and gravelly. He just stood there and looked at Duke. We couldn't see a trace of expression on Jake's face, only the fire flickering on it. Duke got up.

"'Seddown, boy. Here, just let me make a pot of coffee.' He started for his pack.

"'I just killed a man,' Jake said.

"We all froze, and there was quiet again. Corky said something finally. He tried to make it sound offhand. 'Who was it, Jake? You get into a fight or something?'

"'Naw,' Jake said. 'This here is just my night.'

"Corky got up too, and I started to edge back from the fire. 'Your night for what, Jake?' Corky asked.

"'It's just my night.'

"'Watch out!' Corky yelled.

"Duke saw Jake coming, the glint of metal in his hand. He dived just in time. The knife tore through a trailing flap of his jacket. Jake's lunge took him past his target, and before he could get his balance again, Corky's jack-knife went whirling through the air.

"The jack-knife didn't do much damage—the blade caught Jake over the eye, and he started bleeding some, but he turned on Corky who was crouching on the opposite side of the fire. As Jake started to jump Duke came up off the ground with something in his hand. He raised it over his head two-handed and brought it down, hard.

"'Hell!' Corky yelled, 'you got him.'

"'Jake fell into the fire, knocking over the stew, sending sparks blowing upward into the dark.

"I croaked out, 'He's down!'

"'Jesus,' Duke said. Almost in a reflex he bent down and rolled Jake out of the ashes. Corky and I knelt and helped him slap out the spots in Jake's clothes where they had begun to smolder. 'Nutty as a fruitcake,' Duke said. His voice, I noticed, was trembling. 'Looks like he's out cold.'

"Corky looked up. 'He's dead.'

"'Dead!'

"'That two-by-four—it stove in his skull. You must've really bashed him.'

"In the distance there was a diesel horn blowing. The wind was coming up, and a few drops of rain fell sizzling into the embers of the fire. Duke couldn't register it.

"'It'll soon be raining hard,' Corky said. 'We better take care of Jake before we do anything else. Gimme a hand.' I could see Duke was standing there looking for his old answer, but it wouldn't come. This time it wouldn't come. It wouldn't come for me, either, and the three of us split up that night, fast. So here I am," Fairall said. He stopped talking, and there was the sea, underneath it all.

The Gunner's Story

It was the Gunner's mount the sailors were using that night to spin their sea stories on, as the carrier plowed through the star-bitten Pacific, and it was the Gunner's turn.

"Looking back on things," he said, "I guess life had been pretty good, at least for me, until my old man kicked the bucket. I might've even been able to live with that if I hadn't've found out how he died one night when my mother thought I was asleep and got yakking to her best friend, somebody she'd known since she was in school.

"Dad used to take me out to the lake for a day's fishing. We'd float around out there, just dangling our lines and hauling in the black bass. When we got tired we'd lie back in the bottom of our big, flat-bottomed scow, pull our straw hats down over our eyes, and let the sun beat down on us. Man, that was the life. We'd be stripped to the waist and sweating like horses. I could feel the sun soothing the muscles where they ached from being bent over the side of the boat. The smell of the fish we'd caught mixed with the pinewood smell of the scow. It was sort of like a nice form of ether and made me doze off.

"Every now and then a shore breeze would blow by, and we could smell the woods that bordered the lake. The breeze would rumple around our heads for a few minutes, and just as we'd be getting used to it it would stop and the sun would beat down as hard as ever.

"Once in a while a horsefly would buzz around me and finally decide to land. You have to slap 'em fast or they get away and pretty soon come back to pester you again.

"After a while the breezes would start to come up more often and the sides of the boat would block off the sun, and we'd know it was time to go home. Dad would row all the way to shore while I sat and watched the last of the sun glint on his skin. There would be purple splotches in the sky over the wood, and the ripples in the water were gold.

"I was always first out of the scow. I'd sprint over the side, splash into the water, and wade the last few feet to the beach. The sand felt good. And then I'd watch Dad as he got our gear out of the boat and walked toward me. Before he caught up with me I'd stretch till I felt my bones creak, and then lead the way along the path through the woods.

"We had to walk along this pine-needle path to get to Dad's jalopy. Sometimes we'd stop and listen to the wind in the big trees, or look for animals or birds. Sometimes there was a stray bee on its last trip back to the hive.

"But then he died. I was there when they brought him in off the lake. After that I used to have a hard time getting to sleep. I'd go to bed and just lay there listening to my heart pump blood. If my mom checked on me I'd keep my eyes closed and make like I was in Dreamland.

"One night I heard my mother in the hall whispering to somebody, and then she opened the door a crack and I heard her say, 'Doesn't he look cunning, all curled up in bed like that? Oh, you wouldn't believe what an imp he can be sometimes, not when you see him like this, the little angel. You'd never believe he has bad dreams sometimes, poor dear, ever since his dad died in that accident.' I heard her sigh.

"'Poor Sally,' her friend said—I think her name was Smith, Alice Smith. 'You've had a hard life, but it's coming out all right, isn't it? You've hooked another one, haven't you? That's why I dropped in. I'm dying to hear all about it.'

"'Oh, all right,' I heard mom giggle. 'But you've got to promise never to tell anybody. Some people might misunderstand, but I know you won't. I stirred. 'Sshh,' she whispered. "Come into the living room before he wakes up. Honestly, I never get a minute to myself any more. Come on. I'll tell you how I reeled him in.'

"When they closed the door again I got up and snuck out to the hall. I heard them in the living room, so I eased on down to the doorway and listened.

"'Beer?' mom asked, 'or something stronger?"

"'Stronger,' Mrs. Smith said. I chanced a look around the corner and I could see them sitting sideways to me. I could see Alice was all ears. 'What's he like?' she asked.

"'Oh, he's great!' Mom got up to mix martinis. 'He's a big brute of a fella, with fat freckled cheeks and a grin as wide as a pound of bacon. Rrrufff!'

"'Tell me more! Where'd you meet him?' Alice took her drink as mom settled into the scatter pillows on the couch. She rolled her eyes and faked a look around her for spies. I ducked.

"'Don't tell a soul, now promise?' Alice gave a nod full of quick breaths. 'Actually,' mom said in what was supposed to be a low voice, 'I met him before big Mark died. Oh! He swept me right off my feet one day at Danny's Lunch downtown. He just up and sat down at my table—the place was crowded, and the next thing I knew, his knees were nudging me so cute-like while we ate our noodle soup. Oh,' she laughed, 'he's such a card. Just like a little boy, even though he's so big.'

She rolled her eyes again. I sat down on the floor in the hall and didn't look at them any more.

"'Goodness, that's so romantic,' Alice Smith said. I could imagine her teats bobbing and her face flushing. I didn't have to see. 'How I envy you!' she said in little breaths.

"'Till then I'd just been feeling like any old sack. Mark never paid any attention to me, you know. All he ever wanted to do was take junior fishing. Honestly. Two ten-year-olds in the house was too much.' She giggled again and was quiet while she sipped her drink. In the corner the teevee belched and flickered—I could see the shadows coming out into the hall. Then mom said, 'So, while my two boys were out fishing, Harry would come visit me. I fell for him hook, line, and sinker.

"'Well, this went on for about a month. I was getting about ready to get a lawyer when what should happen one day but Mark—big Mark I mean—walked in the door early from work.'

"'No' said Mrs. Smith. I took a quick peek—the one eye I could see was as big and bright as a light bulb.

"'Oh, yes,' said mother, 'and there we were all over the parlor rug, my skirts up around my hips and Harry huffing all over me, snorting like a. . . .'" The Gunner stopped a minute to listen to the sea. Then, "Bull," he said.

"'In a minute it was all over,' mom told Mrs. Smith. 'Mark got all red in the face and Harry got up. He was laughing. Oh, he knows how to take things. He zipped himself up and got ready for a fight.'

"'Then what happened?' I heard Mrs. Smith gasp.

"'Nothing. Mark just walked over to the closet and got his rod and things.'

"'Rod!'

"'Rod and reel.' Mom was quiet for another second. Then, '"I'm going fishing," Mark said. In his business suit, no less. '"In your business suit?" I asked. By this time I was decent again. But he didn't answer. He just walked to the door and out, and that's the last I saw of him.'

"'Alive, anyhow.' I heard mom sip her drink and saw the flare of her lighter as she lit a cigarette. 'After big Mark left, about ten minutes later, maybe, little Mark came in just as Harry was about to leave. He just barely missed us finishing up the job big Mark had interrupted. I think he suspected something anyhow. He gave Harry a funny look and said, "Pop home yet?" I told him he'd gone fishing.

"'Without me?' Then he was out the door like a flash." "I got up and went back to my room then," the Gunner said. "I slammed the door—I didn't give a shit if they heard me. Mom came in. 'What was that door slamming?' she asked me, but I didn't answer. I just kept laying on the bed staring and remembering that day. I don't know how long mom stood there asking me how much I heard, I didn't even do anything when she shook me and bounced me up and down in the bed and slapped me. She finally stopped screaming and crying, and after a while there was the lake again, and it was late in the afternoon. Something was wrong. I'd been running, or maybe pedaling my bike. I don't know how I got to the lake, because it was quite a way—I just knew I had to catch up.

"By the time I was standing on the strip of beach I could feel the night starting to come on—the moon was already up flopping around in the tops of the pines like a sunfish. My legs hurt, and I couldn't breathe—it was like there was water in my chest. I looked for our scow, and it was out there, but there was something funny about it. And then I saw—it was upside-down, and there were a bunch of heads bobbing around it, and another boat. I started in to yell, 'Dad! Dad!' but nobody paid me any attention. Only when I took off my shoes and started to run into the water somebody grabbed me and said, 'Stay here, boy. They'll have him soon.'

"But the moon was high before they brought him in, all soggy, and his eyes staring at me in the dark. His feet were all wound up in line and his metal gear box was caught in the line too. They all just stood around and looked at him, and sometimes they'd look at me too, and then away. I waited for something to happen, but nobody did anything. 'Why don't you all do something? Help him, help him! Jesus!' I said, but they all just shook their heads.

"'It's no use, son. He's been down there for three hours anyway,' somebody said, a cop I think. 'The ambulance will be here soon.'

"But I looked at him and I saw something. 'No, no, he's alive, don't you see?' I said. 'Look, his heart's beating, his heart . . .'

"I managed to rip away from the guy that was holding me, and I fell down beside Dad and put my ear on his chest. I could feel it. His heart thumping, almost jumping out of his chest, trying to keep going. It was slimy wet against my ear, it was wriggling and squirming, even though you could see his face was beginning to bloat and it was all blue. I hugged him and looked up at them all standing around. 'Oh, Jesus, won't you help him!' I screamed. 'Look, his heart!' I tore open his shirt, still with his tie on.

"And you could see it squirming and wiggling, see it with your naked eyes,—a fish caught in his undershirt, a big black bass, fighting to cut loose but losing, its head stuck out near the armpit, its bulgy eyes like two moons staring down at me out of the sky, out of the pines that reeled off into a dark voice that said, 'I wonder what mom will say when we get home for supper.' And then no more dreams, nothing," said the Gunner, "except night and the smell of pine."

"You might be interested to know, Fred, that this last story was the first I ever had published."

"When was that?"

"In 1949. It—or a very early version of it, I should say—won third prize in a high school fiction contest sponsored by my local newspaper."

"Third prize!" Fred sneers. "That's a big deal."

"Actually, it was," the Author says. "The contest was run during the summer before I entered high school, though I was technically a sophomore at the time. I was fifteen."

"I guess we all have to start small."

"Small and early is good."

Fred nods. "The most interesting thing, for me, was seeing how you transcribed a play into a short story. How about the reverse?

"How about a transcription from fiction to cinema of the first of these stories?"

"Okay by me," Fred says, leaning forward to look at the screen."

The Bo'sun's Story, Cinema Version

Scene 1, *Radio music. Opening long shot: panorama of the Pacific Ocean at night from the rail of a ship, an aircraft carrier. The camera rides with the swell, showing the motion of the deck, but this is a big ship and the motion is not violent; nor is the ocean, which is visible under a bright full moon.*

Voice-over (the bo'sun). The Sea's a big fat heart.

The music fades and the soft sound of the sea rises as the camera tracks back to a medium shot of two sailors leaning over the rail. The big man to the left is speaking. He is the bo'sun. There is a cigarette in his left hand; we can see the glow. Behind them a hatch opens and spreads light over the steel deck underfoot. The camera tracks sideways to include in the shot the gun shack where seven sailors lie and sit or pour coffee into the big cups, or play cards. The hatch swings to again, and the night closes once more around the gun mount.

Close-up: *The bo'sun turns so that he is in profile facing his companion who doesn't move.*

Bo'sun. It was in them Oklahoma nights that I heard her pounding first. I guess you'll say I'm nuts to think I heard the sea beating under a lot of red clay. But that's the way it was. I can even remember the first night I figured out what it was there off in the distance, just whispering like, at the edges.

The bo'sun drags on his cigarette, then flips the butt overboard. The camera follows the arc of its fall a little way.

Bo'sun. I'd went upstairs early that night when my pa come home drunk. We owned a farm, or the bank did. It was the first day of the month, and ma and me knew he'd come home smashed into a buzzard's tail. He always did the day the bank payment was due. In the morning of such a day we'd all rise hard out of our beds and drag downstairs. Everything was a coat of dust. You got so you didn't notice it usually, but on these days the dust would sift in with the moonlight, I guess, through sashes and panes, and in your nose it would make a smell like rust that you couldn't wash down even with a cup of mucky coffee.

Fade to scene 2: the kitchen of a run-down farmhouse. A man and a boy sitting at the table, being served by a woman in an apron.

Voice-over (the bo'sun). We would rise up and go down to sit at the table, quiet, while ma made the breakfast. She would serve it, and pa wouldn't say nothing, just sit there squint-eyed and hard, thinking about the money.

You don't raise much on a little Oklahoma farm, no matter how hard you scratch. It wasn't pa's fault, you just don't raise much. And the bank don't know nothing about wheat or corn or swine or drought, or the red dust and the wind.

The action in the kitchen continues. The man finishes and rises.

Man. That damn wind! It never stops. Almost never. *(He goes to the door and looks through the screening.)* In the morning it blows outta the east, strong enough to lean against sometimes, and the dry mud blows over from miles gone. *(He shakes his head and wipes his face with a big handkerchief.)* At noon it quits for a breather, just long enough for the sun to bake the land flat again. Then it starts all over, outta the west this time, and the countryside blows past again, back where it came from. *(He turns to face the woman at the sink now.)*

That dirt never settles long enough to grow anything. Even when it gets wet with a hard rain all you have is a foot of mud with hardpan underneath.

Woman. And then the mud just runs off into the creeks until there's a drought and the creeks dry up.

Man. Then the wind blows it all back up again. You can't grow nothing but weary on land like this.

He sits back down at the table and pulls out his wallet. The boy gets up and goes out on the front steps. The woman looks over her shoulder at the man who starts taking greenbacks out of his wallet. He looks at each one for a moment then slaps them down on the table. The only sound besides the bills hitting the table is the sound of the wind.

Voice-over (the bo'sun). When he was done counting he gathered them all back up, rose, stuffed them in his pocket, and put his wallet back away.

Man. I'm goin' into town.

He gets up and goes out. The camera follows the action in the house as the woman and the boy go about their business, she cleaning up and he toting in wood.

Voice-over (the bo'sun). *(Light-hearted background music)* He'd be gone all day. I'd have some time to myself if it wasn't a school day, so I'd spend my time out in the fields or the brush woods. *(The camera follows the boy in his wanderings and actions.)* I remember I had a pet horn-toad named Sam. I would gather him up and put him in my shirt pocket head down. He'd stay there that way or, if I put him in tail first, he'd look around a while and then get out and crawl around on my shoulders *(Close-up of a horned toad looking out of a shirt pocket)*. I fed him flies from the barn, or put a string leash on him and let him forage on his own. I did other things to kill time, I guess, but that's the thing I remember best.

The day would be over some time, though, and I'd make my excuses to get to bed before pa got home. *(Background music becomes darker, more ominous.)* My ma would nod as she sat by the kitchen stove darning or something, and it was then that I felt sorriest, for I knew she'd have to wait up till he got home, and he'd beat the shit out of her. He never did that any time but the one night a month, but I hated his pus gut for that.

The camera stays on the boy as he putters around in his room and eventually gets ready for bed. There are sounds from downstairs occasionally.

Voice-over (the bo'sun). It wasn't for years that I figured out why she'd wait like that, just rocking and darning, till he cracked open the door and smashed her across the face with his open hand. She was a little woman, but not sickly little. She'd wait, and when he'd come in she'd look up at him scared some, but a funny glint in her eyes. *(We hear the sounds from downstairs.)*

Man. You done this to me! You've bought my spirit for a pound of flesh and crucified my heart with a son. You've got this coming, you and womankind. *(We hear the sounds of the beating, but the camera stays on the boy who curls up into a fetal position in his bed and puts the pillow over his head.)*

Voice-over (the bo'sun). He hit her till she laid crying on the linoleum tiles. I thought I could even smell the liquor floating up the stairs. And then he'd lift her and take her off to bed. *(We hear the sounds of footsteps on the stairs)* where he'd pound her belly against the sheets, and her cries would be different, but just as fearful. Or worse. Because now you could hear the pleasure in them. *(We hear everything. The camera tracks to the window as the sounds fade and go to another long shot of the sky and the stars).*

Then the house would settle down into the red dark, and the plains and fields would begin to whisper to the walls. In my bed my toad would settle into my side, but I would listen for the sounds of the dust riding moonlight sliding through the windows. Out of the stars the wind would begin to come up stronger—you'd know what it felt like if you tried, to be a limb of a tree creaking in the night.

But under it all there was a strange sound, like wet things sliding over each other, and strange animals walking on the bottom of things. First far off, making a roar just under your eyelid, then slimming off, then a roar again—if you didn't listen you didn't know it was there, not with your whole mind. And a smell, a smell from way back and way down deep. And then one night I remembered that it was the sea, and I'd never rest until I saw it. Then sleep took me with my eyes stark open, and I heard my mother sigh once from her dark covers before I dropped off the quiet edge." *(Music down. Sounds of the sea.)*

The camera fades to black and comes up again on the shipboard scene and the backs of the two sailors leaning over the rail. The sounds of the sea fade, fade-out.

"Man, that's dark," Fred says.

"Actually, it would probably be shot in the style called film noir."

"You've got a lot of different terms in this filmscript," Fred notes.

"They're all in *The Book of Literary Terms* if you want to look them up."

Fred squints at the Author. "Did you ever consider that maybe you write too much? Or that other writers might not like you for giving away all the secrets of the trade?"

"No and yes," the Author says.

"Well, then, how about a television script. Would it be different from a movie script?"

"Not much. But we have one more little tale in *Shipmates*. Let's turn 'The Gunner's Story' into a teleplay, only this time we'll do it without a voice-over narrator":

The Gunner's Story, Teleplay

Scene 1, establishing shot: *camera tracks down a suburban street, pivots to a home, fades through the front door to a medium shot of two women, Sally and Alice, standing in the upstairs hall, outside a bedroom door. Sally is a good-looking blonde woman of about thirty-five; her friend, Joan, is a brunette of about the same age. Sally puts her finger to her lips and speaks softly to her friend.*

Sally. Let me take a look at him and then we can go downstairs and talk.

She opens the door a crack; the camera tracks in over their shoulders to a close-up of a boy seemingly sleeping in his bed.

Sally. Doesn't he look cunning, all curled up in bed like that? Oh, you wouldn't believe what an imp he can be sometimes, not when you see him like this, the little angel. You'd never believe he has bad dreams sometimes, poor dear, ever since his dad died in that boating accident.

Alice. Poor Sally! You've had a hard life, but it's coming out all right, isn't it? You've hooked another one, haven't you? That's why I dropped in. I'm dying to hear all about it.

(Sally pulls the door to, but just before the camera follows them down the hall we see the boy's eyes open.)

Sally. Oh, all right. *(She giggles.)* But you've got to promise never to tell anybody. Some people might misunderstand, but I know you won't. *(They hear something in the boy's room and pause.)* Sshh! Come into the living room before he wakes up. Honestly, I never get a minute to myself any more. Come on. I'll tell you how I reeled in the new one.

The camera picks them up as they walk into the living room, then travels back up the stairs where we see the boy settling in to listen at the top of the stairs, out of the line of sight of the women.

Sally. Beer, or something stronger?

Alice. Stronger!

Sally goes out of the room for a moment and comes back in with a cocktail shaker.

Sally. Martinis okay? I had these cooling.

Alice. Martinis are fine. What's he like?

Sally. Oh, he's great! *(She pours the martinis and serves Alice one.)* He's a big brute of a fella, with fat freckled cheeks and a grin as wide as a pound of bacon. Rrrufff!

Alice. Tell me more! Where'd you meet him? *(Alice takes her drink as Sally settles into the scatter pillows on the couch. She rolls her eyes and fakes a look around her for spies. At the top of the stairs we see the boy duck, but he needn't have worried.)*

Sally. Don't tell a soul, now promise? *(Alice nods eagerly.)* Actually, I met him before big Mark died. Oh! He swept me right off my feet one day at Danny's Lunch downtown. He just up and sat down at my table—the place was crowded, and the next thing I knew, his knees were nudging me so cute-like while we ate our noodle soup. Oh *(she laughs),* he's such a card. Just like a little boy, even though he's so big. She rolls her eyes.

(In the hall upstairs the boy turns his back on the women. He continues to listen, but he no longer looks at them.)

Alice. Goodness, that's so romantic! How I envy you!

Sally. Till then I'd just been feeling like any old sack. Mark never paid any attention to me, you know. All he ever wanted to do was take junior fishing. Honestly. Two ten-year-olds in the house was too much. *(She giggles again and is quiet while she sips her drink. In the corner the teevee belches and flickers, but the sound is off.)* So, while my two boys are out fishing, Harry would come visit me. I fell for him hook, line, and sinker.

Well, this went on for about a month. I was getting about ready to get a lawyer when what should happen one day but Mark—big Mark I mean—walked in the door early from work.

Alice. No!

Sally. Oh, yes, and there we were all over the parlor rug, my skirts up around my hips and Harry huffing all over me, snorting like a bull!

In a minute it was all over. Mark got all red in the face and Harry got up. He was laughing. Oh, he knows how to take things. He zipped himself up and got ready for a fight.

Alice. *(Gasps)* Then what happened?

Sally. Nothing. Mark just walked over to the closet and got his rod and things.

Alice. Rod!

Sally. Rod and reel. *(She is quiet while she finishes her martini.)* Then he says, "I'm going fishing."

Alice. Fishing!

Sally. In his business suit, no less! "In your business suit?" I ask. By this time I was decent again. But he didn't answer. He just walks to the door and out, and that's the last I saw of him.

Alive, anyhow. *(She pours Alice and herself another drink and lights a cigarette with a table lighter.)* After big Mark left, about ten minutes later, maybe, little Mark came in just as Harry was about to leave. He just barely missed us finishing up the job big Mark had interrupted. I think he suspected something anyhow. He gave Harry a funny look and said, "Pop home yet?" I told him he'd gone fishing.

"Without me?" Then he was out the door like a flash.

There is the sound upstairs of a door slamming. The camera stays on the women, who flinch.

Sally. Oh, god! I hope he wasn't listening!

She gets up and goes quickly up the stairs, down the hall, and into the boy's room.

Sally. What was that door slamming?

She shakes the boy on the bed, but he doesn't answer, just lies on the bed star-ing. She shakes him some more, screaming and crying, and bounces him up and down in the bed, then she slaps him. He doesn't respond. The camera tracks away from the vignette and into his eyes.

Scene 2, flashback to a lake, late on a summer afternoon. The boy jumps off his bike at a little pier. He drops it and runs down to the water. The night is begin-ning to come on as he looks out at an overturned scow, a bunch of heads bobbing around it, and another boat.

Boy. Dad! Dad! *(No one pays any attention. He takes off his shoes and starts to run into the water. A bystander grabs him.)*

Bystander. Stay here, boy. They'll have him soon.

The camera angle is panoramic on the sun going down. Fade out and back up on the moon risen on the horizon. The boy is sitting on the beach crying as the res-cuers bring in the body all soggy, and its eyes staring in the semi-dark. Its feet are wound up in fishing line a metal gear box is caught in the line too. Everyone just stands around looking at him while the emergency crew attempts CPR. Now and again someone would look at the boy too, and then away.

Boy. Why don't you all do something? Help him, help him! Jesus!

The bystander, who still has a hand on the boy's shoulder, just shakes his head.

Bystander. It's no use, son. He's been down there for three hours anyway.

Policeman. The ambulance will be here soon.

Boy. *(Trying to pull away.)* No, no, he's alive, don't you see? Look, his heart's beating, his heart. . . .

He manages to rip away from the man who is holding him. He falls down beside his father and puts his ear on his chest. He hugs the body and looks up at the people standing around.

Boy. Oh, Jesus, won't you help him! Look, his heart!

Close-up: he tears open his father's shirt, still with his tie on, to expose a fish caught in his undershirt, a big black bass, fighting to get loose its head sticking out near the armpit.

Boy. I wonder what mom will say when we get home for supper.

Blackout.

"You wrote that when you were fifteen?" Fred asks, a note of incredulity in his voice.

"The only part of the story that was written when I was that young is the description of the fishing trip in the original version."

"Right," Fred replies. "No way that gets into a family newspaper as it stands now."

"What can I say? When you're right, you're right."

"What haven't we done," Fred asks, "in the way of scripts?"

"Well, one section of 'Shipmates' started out as a play, 'Barrow Yard,' and we adapted it as a vignette, 'The Yeoman's Story'; we adapted a vignette, 'The Bo'sun's Story,' as a screenplay, and we did the same for 'The Gunner's Story' as a teleplay. Maybe we could finish up by turning 'The Yeoman's Story' back into a radioplay, meant to be heard only and not seen."

The Yeoman's Story, Radioplay

Music. Theme. Fadeaway.

Announcer. And now for our Radio Theater presentation, "The Yeoman's Story," by Fred Foyle. *(The music fades further as the sound of the ocean rises in the background.)* It is a warm night. We are standing on the deck of a gunmount on the U.S.S. *Hornet* (CVA 12), an aircraft carrier cruising the Straits of Formosa in 1954. Two sailors, a Yeoman 3rd class named Fairall, and another whose name we don't know are leaning on the port rail of the mount drinking coffee. Behind them a hatch opens and we can see into the gun shack where the sailors on duty are playing cards and listening to the radio. *(Pop music rises briefly, then the hatch closes—we hear it clank shut. The sounds of the sea again.)* Fairall is the only one talking.

Yeoman Fairall. I ran away from home when I was sixteen. I hadn't been on the road long before I fell in with an old hobo named Duke, a younger one named Corky, and Jake. I don't know how to describe Jake. Duke had some education, but he wouldn't talk much about his past. I had to pry it out of him over a period of time.

One night he sat looking into the fire and he said to himself for the umpteen-thousandth time, "It's logical." He always began by being amazed at his presence in a place like that—an abandoned brickyard on the outskirts of some town somewhere on the prairies, or in the South, or anywhere else. But when he'd asked himself how he'd gotten where he was and had retraced his route from its beginning to a particular campfire, he always ended by saying the same thing: "it's logical. " Duke was proud of only one thing—that his mind hadn't deteriorated, like about everything else, over the years.

He raised his eyes from the fire. In the falling dusk we could see the walls of the old brickworks surrounding us, the caved-in stacks of brick, pretty well raided by the population of the dying town, the faded lettering painted on the side of a broken-down building that formed one side of the place. It read, "BARROW YARD, BRICKS AND BUILDING MATERIALS *WHOLESALE ONLY.*"

Duke dropped his eyes to the fire again, and I could see he was letting his mind walk back along that old road. There was the growing up, in good shape, in Illinois—a small city near Chicago just before the war. He had had some ambition then. And there had been the couple of years of college before Pearl Harbor. It looked like he was going someplace in those days—his father's small factory was waiting for him. Elise was waiting for him, too.

Elise had still been waiting for him when he got back from the Pacific, but there had been no time to finish his degree, because of his father's death in 'forty-four, just before Duke's return. And there'd been the business slump that hit a few marginal industries during the shift to a post-war economy. The plant, engaged in war work for a few years, had put its profits into expansion, and when the fighting ended there was nothing left to pump into another changeover. Duke was under a lot of pressure in those days, and he hadn't been very well prepared to walk out of Guam and the Philippines into Illinois and take on the job of saving the family firm.

No wonder his marriage hadn't lasted, especially after Elise miscarried their first child. After that it had been a steep slope downhill for Duke—business failure, his mother's broken health and her death grieving over the smash of everything. She'd had only the one son.

Then the heavy drinking for a few years, and the waking, one morning, to find himself staring into the flames of the first campfire and asking himself how he had gotten where he was. And, of course, the answer.

Duke. It's logical.

Corky. What is?

Fairall. Duke looked up to see Corky approaching the fire with a stack of wood. Corky dropped the pile nearby *(sounds of wood falling)* and squatted to warm his hands.

Corky. Man, that fire feels good. What's logical?

Fairall. Corky was heavy, dressed in jeans and an old leather jacket. Corky's presence was logical too—he was on the run from something, none of us had bothered to ask what. We didn't want to know. Duke lifted a hand to run it over his face, rough with stubble, thin and hollow. He shrugged.

Duke. Us. We're what's logical.

Fairall. Corky grunted *(a grunt),* like he always did. I guess it irritated him when Duke went into his memory routine.

Corky. Not to change the subject, but when's Jake going to show, I wonder? He'd been gone a long time. Maybe one of us should've gone with him.

Fairall. Duke shrugged again.

Duke. He'll be back.

Corky. I sure hope he brings some grub.

Fairall. Corky liked to talk, but he was quiet for a time, and we watched the fire crackle *(sound effects)* and cast strange figures into the dusk and the thin mist that was settling on Barrow Yard.

Corky. I've got a feeling we better not wait. I got a surprise I been saving.

Fairall. Corky got up, went over toward the gate of the Yard, and came back with a paper bag. He squatted and opened it. *(sounds of paper rustling)*

Corky. I ran across a truck garden while I was out looking for wood.

Fairall. We looked in and saw vegetables—carrots, cabbages, celery, some small potatoes.

Duke. Not bad.

Fairall. Duke reached over to his pack and got the pan he always carried, and a box of salt *(sound effects)*.

Duke. There's a stream near here. I'll get some water and you start on the vegetables.

Fairall. Duke got up and went through the gate. It was still barely light enough for him to make his way down to the woods, but he had to go carefully. By the time he got back Corky and I had finished paring. Duke arranged the pan in the fire, salted the water, and we threw in the vegetables *(sound effects)*. We sat awhile smelling the aroma that started to rise from the stew.

Corky. Man, that Jake is slow. And dumb. I hope be brings some meat. There's times I wish we hadn't of gone and let him feed with us that night.

Duke. You know damn well there's not a thing we could've done about it. He saw our fire, and then there he was, standing in the light. Probably be the same thing tonight. He'll stand there saying nothing till we invite him over. It's sure strange, the way he acts.

Corky. Yeah, but you got to admit he's got a lot of guts. Remember the fight in the freight yard when that yard man found us outside Denver? That boy's all right in a pinch.

Duke. Knock if off. I think I hear him coming.

Fairall. We listened. From the direction of the woods there were noises in the brush, hard and fast *(sound effects)*. Corky looked up.

Corky. He's sure making a racket. Hell, I think he's running.

Fairall. The crackling noises stopped, and we could hear heavy footsteps slowing down *(sound of steps approaching),* coming across the packed dirt of the Yard, but it was too dark by then to see much. Then there was that huge man in the glow of the fire. He took a couple of steps forward.

Corky. *(Loud whisper.)* He's making straight for you, Duke.

Fairall. We saw Jake stop and gaze down at Duke who got to feeling uncomfortable after a while.

Duke. *(Clears his throat.)* Hi, Jake. he said. Dig in and grab a little stew, boy. Looks as though you've worked up a sweat. Do you good to smoke a butt and sit down for a while. Where you been?

Jake. In town.

Fairall. Jake's voice was thick and gravelly. He just stood there and looked at Duke. We couldn't see a trace of expression on Jake's face, only the fire flickering on it. Duke got up.

Duke. Seddown, boy. Here, just let me make a pot of coffee.

Jake. I just killed a man.

Fairall. We all froze, and there was quiet again. Corky said something finally. He tried to make it sound offhand.

Corky. Who was it, Jake? You get into a fight or something?

Jake. Naw. This here is just my night.

Fairall. Corky got up too, and I started to edge back from the fire.

Corky. Your night for what, Jake?

Jake. It's just my night.

Corky. Watch out, Duke!

Fairall. Duke saw Jake coming, the glint of metal in his hand. *(Fast and over-lapping sound effects.)* He dived just in time. The knife tore through a trailing flap of his jacket. Jake's lunge took him past his target, and before he could get his balance again, Corky's jack-knife went whirling through the air.

The jack-knife didn't do much damage—the blade caught Jake over the eye, and he started bleeding some, but he turned on Corky who was crouching on the opposite side of the fire. As Jake started to jump, Duke came up off the ground with something in his hand. He raised it over his head two-handed and brought it down, hard *(Sound of a hard blow, wood on flesh)*.

Corky. Hell! You got him.

Fairall. Jake fell into the fire, knocking over the stew, sending sparks blowing upward into the dark *(Sound effects)*. I croaked out, "He's down!"

Duke. Jesus! Help me roll him out of the fire.

Fairall. Corky and I knelt and helped him slap out the spots in Jake's clothes where they had begun to smolder *(Sounds of slapping clothing)*.

Duke. *(Voice trembling.)* Nutty as a fruitcake, Looks like he's out cold.

Corky. He's dead.

Duke. Dead!

Corky. That two-by-four—it stove in his skull. You must've really bashed him.

Fairall. In the distance there was a diesel horn blowing *(Sound effects).* The wind was coming up, and a few drops of rain fell sizzling into the embers of the fire. Duke couldn't register it.

Corky. It'll soon be raining hard. We better take care of Jake before we do anything else. Gimme a hand.

Fairall. I could see Duke was standing there looking for his old answer, but it wouldn't come. This time it wouldn't come. It wouldn't come for me, either, and the three of us split up that night, fast. So here I am.

(Sound of the ocean up, then fade-away to silence. Theme music up.)

Announcer. And that was our Radio Theater presentation, "The Yeoman's Story," by Fred Foyle. The cast was *(List of dramatis personae).* Join us again next week, same time, same station, for another installment of your Radio Theater. *(Music down and out.)*

Chapter 5

Genre Dialogue

"What's left?" Fred asks.

"Well," says the Author, sezee, "we haven't specifically discussed dialogue as it's used in genre writing, although we've mentioned several genres, and we have examples of dialogue as it's used in some of those."

Fantasy

"Such as?" Fred Foyle leans forward in the La-Z-Boy and casts his eyes toward the ceiling, as though he were trying to remember some genres. "Wait!" he says, "I recall some things. You mentioned J. R. R. Tolkien's *Lord of the Rings,* and you pointed out that he used a slightly elevated diction and a formal syntax to indicate an invented archaic language."

"Something like that," the Author replies. "But every case will be different and require its own adjustments in approach."

Fred nods. "I can see that. After all, 'Scot on the Rocks' was a sort of fantasy, and you had to adjust in several ways for that—the pseudo-Scots dialect, the somewhat formal diction of Holmesby. . . ."

Science Fiction

"And *Dune* is science fiction. For the most part," the Author points out, "writers are going to use standard American or standard British when they write with particular adjustments in grammar, syntax, and diction for particular characters. Here's a bit from Harry Bates' science-fiction story, 'A Matter of Size'":

The ethologist, becoming aware that Miss So-and-So had said "How do you do!" in the most conventional of Earth fashions, in turn nodded and mumbled something himself. Jones smiled broadly and, stepping to the door, begged to be excused, saying he was overwhelmed with work.

"Miss CB-301 speaks your language perfectly," he said, "and will explain such things as are permitted. I'll be back presently." And the door clicked closed behind him. . . .

What should he say to the female? Nice day? No—better, flattery. He complimented her on the lack of accent in her speech. It suggested unusual brains in one so young.

"Oh, but no—I'm really terribly dumb!" the young thing gushed sincerely. "I could hardly get through my fourth-dimensional geometry! But English is easier. Don't you think so?"

"I see what you mean—she's differentiated by breathiness and gushiness, but not by accent or anything unusual in her verbal constructions."

Juveniles

"Right," the Author agrees, "and that'll even hold true for juveniles that are fantasies. Here's a short segment of the novel *Watership Down* by the English author Richard Adams. The speakers are rabbits":

Bigwig, crouched close to Blackberry in the straw of the cattle shed, leaped to flight at the sound of the shot two hundred yards up the lane. He checked himself and turned to the others.

"Don't run!" he said quickly. "Where do you want to run to, anyway? No holes here."

"Further away from the gun," replied Blackberry, white-eyed.

"Wait!" said Bigwig, listening. "They're running down the lane. Can't you hear them?"

"I can hear only two rabbits," answered Blackberry, after a pause. "and one of them sounds exhausted."

"But this is a novel for older children, isn't it?" Fred asks, riffling through the pages. "It looks as though even adults could enjoy it."

Repetition

"It was a huge best-seller in the United States when it was published in the early 'seventies," the Author says. "But there's not a huge adjustment to make, even for younger children. A writer doesn't have to condescend to them, just be clear and uncomplicated, as in drama. Furthermore, one mustn't be afraid of repetition—kids love hearing a story over and over again, and they learn that way."

"What way?"

"By hearing the main points or foreshadowings, or whatever it may be, more than one time during the course of the story. Here's a whole children's story, a sequel titled 'Murgatroyd Tries Again' by 'Wesli Court.' That's a pen-name, by the way."

"Whose?"

"Figure it out. The original story was about two caterpillars, both of whom built cocoons, but only one of whom—Mabel—emerged at first seemingly unchanged, until they realized that he's grown a propeller instead":

Murgatroyd Tries Again

Murgatroyd and Mabel were butterflies. That is to say, Mabel was a butterfly, but Murgatroyd was still a caterpillar, in a way. They had both been caterpillars once. Murgatroyd had been a sort of spring green in color, with bright orange spots. Mabel had been covered with soft brown fur, and she had two pretty yellow tufts on her head, like a hat.

Then, one day, Murgatroyd and Mabel had spun their cocoons, and when they came out Mabel had worn two lovely lavender wings on her slender pink body. But when he came out, Murgatroyd looked just the same as before. He still looked like a caterpillar, except for one thing. Instead of growing wings, Murgratroyd had grown a propeller on his nose.

Murgatroyd could fly very fast with his propeller, and he could do loops and other tricks. "I wish I could fly like that," Mabel told him, and that made him happy. As Mabel would flutter by, Murgatroyd did barrel rolls and loop-the-loops around her so that they could get where they were going at the same time.

But one day as Murgatroyd and Mabel were sitting on a green twig in an apple tree he said to his friend, "Mabel, I think I'd like to try again."

Mabel was quite puzzled. "What do you mean?" she asked him, waving her wings delicately in the summer breeze.

Murgatroyd spun his propeller a little bit. "I'd like to try to grow wings again," he said.

"Oh, I see," Mabel said. "But you fly very well. Why would you want to do that?"

"Just to see if I can do it," Murgatroyd replied.

"You'll have to spin another cocoon, then," Mabel said.

"That's just what I had in mind," Murgatroyd said, and then and there he began to spin a new cocoon on the apple tree twig. Mabel sat and watched, and when he was through he poked his head out of the door of his cocoon and said, "I'll see you in eleven days."

"I'll be waiting," Mabel said, and Murgatroyd closed the door.

The sun rose and set ten times, and ten days passed, but there was hardly a sound in the apple tree except when a robin perched near the cocoons to look out over the green fields. On the eleventh day, though, something began to happen to the cocoon. Slowly, slowly, the door opened, but it was so dark inside that Mabel could see nothing at all.

Then, at last, Murgatroyd came out—only, he didn't look exactly as

Mabel remembered. When he had come all the way out and stood on the apple tree twig Mabel said, "Oh, Murgatroyd! It didn't work! And, and. . . ."

Murgatroyd looked down the length of his body, but it seemed to be just as it had been before he went into the cocoon. He looked at Mabel and said, "And what?"

Mabel felt very sad. "And you've even lost your propeller. Now you won't be able to fly at all."

Murgatroyd crossed his eyes to look at his nose, and, sure enough, the propeller was gone! "Oh, no!" he said. "I should have left well enough alone!" He was so dejected that he forgot to hold on to the twig, and he fell off.

"Murgatroyd!" Mabel cried, but there was nothing she could do. He was heading for the ground lickety-split. Then, suddenly, something happened. There was a roar, a blast of flame, and just as he was about to hit the ground Murgatroyd began to climb into the sky leaving a vapor trail behind him.

Mabel watched as her friend roared through the branches of the apple tree and disappeared into the sun, and she was still watching when Murgatroyd reappeared in a flash and settled onto the twig beside her.

"What was that?" she asked him.

"Look at me again," Murgatroyd said. "Don't you see?"

Mabel looked at him very closely, and then she saw it—Murgatroyd had lost his propeller, and he hadn't grown wings, but he had grown a jet pod instead!

"Oh, Murgatroyd," Mabel laughed, fluttering her lavender wings as she flew away from the apple twig. "You're twice as fast as you were before!" But Murgatroyd had no time to answer, for it was all he could do to shout "Whee!" as he did power dives and triple barrel rolls around her in the sweet summer air.

"That sounds nothing at all like Brer Rabbit," Fred says. "There's not a whole lot of difference between it and ordinary standard English except for the repetitions."

"And the simple declarative sentences with their uncomplicated syntactical constructions. The level of diction is mean, and the whole story is built for hearing, not just the dialogue."

"I get the idea," Fred tucks his chin into his hand and leans over the shoulder of the Author. "I notice the story stays away from colloquialisms and idiomatic expressions, too. Now—" he steps back and stretches—"what other genres have we got to talk about?"

Romances

"Let's take a look at a romance by Danielle Steel . . . it's from her novel *Crossings.*"

"Anything in particular I ought to be looking for?"

"Yes. Notice how she uses those things you just said were left out of the children's story—colloquialisms and idiomatic expressions—and how she keeps the action going simultaneously with the conversation. While Hillary, in a hotel in Cannes, is talking with her husband on the phone, she is also interacting with her lover":

"Sorry to bother you, Hil."

"Is something wrong?" The thought instantly crossed her mind that something had happened to Johnny, and as she walked naked across Philip Markham's room, holding the phone, her face wore a nervous expression. She glanced guiltily at him over her shoulder and then turned away as she waited for Nick's answer.

"Have you read the papers yesterday or today?"

"You mean that thing about the Germans and the Russians?"

"Yes, that's exactly what I mean."

"Oh, for chrissake, Nick. I thought something had happened to Johnny." She almost sighed with relief as she sat on a chair and Philip began to stroke her leg as she smiled at him.

"He's fine. But I want you to come home."

"You mean now?"

"Yes. That's exactly what I mean."

"Why? I was coming home next week anyway."

"That may not be soon enough."

"For what?" She thought he was being a nervous fool, and she laughed as she watched Philip make funny faces and make obscene gestures as he returned to their freshly rumpled bed.

"I think there's going to be a war. They're mobilizing the French army, and things are liable to explode any day."

"Lots of action there," Fred notes.

"Both physical and verbal," the Author agrees.

"And Steel slows it down as little as possible—there aren't even tag lines in the passage you quote, and even though three people are in on the action, the reader is never confused about who is doing or saying what." Fred smiles. He is clearly delighted.

Action Fiction

"No doubt," he continues, "the same is true for adventure stories or spy novels."

"Let's check it out," the Author says. "Robert Ludlum in *The Bourne Conspiracy* uses tremendous amounts of dialogue. There are whole pages of it, with just a line or two of narration in between the speeches":

"Who sent you?" asked the Oriental of mixed blood, as he sat down.

"Move away from the edge. I want to talk very quietly."

"Yes, of course." Jiang Yu inched his way directly opposite Bourne. "I must ask. Who sent you?"

"I must ask," said Jason, "do you like American movies? Especially our Westerns?"

"Of course. American films are beautiful, and I admire the movies of your old West most of all. So poetic in retribution, so righteously violent. Am I saying the correct words?"

"Yes, you are. Because right now you're in one."

"I beg your pardon?"

"I have a very special gun under the table. It's aimed between your legs." Within the space of a second, Jason held back the cloth, pulled up the weapon so the barrel could be seen, and immediately shoved the gun back into place. "It has a silencer that reduces the sound of a forty-five to the pop of a champagne cork, but not the impact. Liao jie ma?"

"Liao jie . . ." said the Oriental, rigid, breathing deeply in fear.

Rhythm

"That conversation just seems to rip along," Fred says. "How is it that you haven't talked about the rhythms of dialogue? Shouldn't you have said something about that back when we were discussing pace?

The Author sits back and stares at the computer monitor for a few moments. "I've been putting it off," he says.

"Why?"

"Because what you just said—that the 'conversation just seems to rip along'—is about as much as most people who write about dialogue say, only they tend to use the word 'flow'—the dialogue is supposed to 'flow.'"

"What's wrong with that?"

"What's wrong is that to say so is to say nothing. Anyone ought to know that dialogue should run along like water and keep the reader's attention. The problem is that water can 'flow' in hundreds of ways. It can move gently toward the sea; it can dash through rapids; it can roar over cataracts, or it can be as majestic as the Mississippi."

The Author is just warming up. "A writer can learn the rhythms of speech in two ways, it seems to me. By trial and error one can develop an 'ear' for dialogue, or one can study language formally and learn abut its rhythms the way a poet learns, by 'scanning' it and developing an ear according to a program of study."

"What do you mean, an 'ear'?" Fred asks.

"J. D. Salinger's *A Catcher in the Rye* is one of the best-selling books of all time. Here's one of the reasons why—Holden Caulfield says, 'What really knocks me out is a book that, when you're all done reading it, you wish the author that wrote it was a terrific friend of yours and you could call him up on the phone whenever you felt like it.' That's not very good grammatically or syntactically. It's not what one would call 'realistic' in the sense that it's verisimilitudinous dialogue . . ."

("Ye gods!" Fred whispers to himself.)

". . . but what it is is absolutely accurate. Every American teenager who loves to read will probably recognize it as his or her own speech—but more than that, as his or her own *thoughts verbalized.*"

"I see that," Fred says. "You mean it's psychologically and linguistically accurate."

"And appropriate to the character as well. Everything works. It's as though Salinger had reached into the reader's brain, pulled out his or her own thoughts, and put them into the mouth of a character that the reader recognizes as himself or herself. That is an ear. Perhaps one can be born having the talent to write like that," the Author says, shaking his head, "but I think it's more likely Salinger spent a lot of time listening to the way people—especially young people—talk, and then a lot more time trying to get it right on paper.

"And there are all kinds of rhythms, too," the Author continues.

"What do you mean?"

"I mean, sometimes you don't want language to 'flow.' For instance, if you have a person, let's say, who is out of breath, you're going to want to do something like this, perhaps":

"Oh!" she gasped, "that man—help! My purse . . . he took it! Please! Stop him. Stop him!" she screamed.

"Dialogue should never look composed," the Author continues, "it ought not to look as though it's been written. What you want is to approach the Salinger ideal: dialogue ought to appear to be overheard.

"So that's what you'd recommend?" Fred asks.

"The Author nods emphatically. "Listen and write, and study the craft."

The two of them—the Author and the would-be-writer—sit quietly for a few minutes listening to Debussy's "La Mer" issuing dreamily from the speakers and, under it, the hum of the air conditioner.

Summing Up

"Okay, Fred," the Author says at last, "let's see if you've been listening. What are some of the things you've learned or figured out?"

"Final exam time?" Fred grins.

"Orals."

Variation

"Right. Well, for one thing I think one needs to break up dialogue at strategic places, especially monologues."

"How?"

"With action, with the short remarks, replies, or interjections of other characters, with scene-setting and atmosphere—almost anything that's relevant to the story."

"Fine. Anything else?"

Personal Address

"Don't use people's names too often. In real life people don't continually address each other by name. When they greet each other on meeting, I notice, they may say, 'Hello, John,' or 'Hi, Mary,' but after that, they stop using their names. For instance, this is an unnatural conversation":

"Gee, John, I haven't seen you in a month of Sundays."
"No, where have you been keeping yourself, Mary."
"Well, I'll tell you, John, I've not been well."
"Oh, Mary! I'm sorry to hear it."
"I'm better now, John. No need to worry."
"I'm certainly glad to hear that, Mary."

"Good point," the Author says. "If your concern is that the reader will lose track of who's speaking, figure out other ways of tipping them off. Tag lines are the simplest expedient. But generally it's not hard to know who's speaking if the characterizations and situations are clear."

Subtlety

"And be subtle in the way you introduce background information such as scene-setting and exposition. Don't put it all into someone's mouth," Fred says. "Get as much of that sort of thing worked into the fabric and action of the story as possible, and if you have to, just be straight about it. Do it and get it over with."

"Any examples?"

"Sure," Fred says. "Remember all that stuff about the 'scientific' qualities of ectoplasm that you had in 'Scot on the Rocks'? I guess stuff like that has to be done in science fiction sometimes, and I think I liked it better when you just explained it than I would have if you'd tried to disguise it as dialogue or something like that—though it was still pretty heavy-handed at that."

Summary Dialogue

"And stay away from summary dialogue, if possible," the Author says.

"Have we talked about that?"

"Yes, when we discussed 'describing' dialogue instead of writing it out":

"Where have you been?" he asked, and he spent the next ten minutes listening to her talk about her latest operation, the five days she had spent in the hospital, and all the pain and discomfort she had felt and was, for that matter, still feeling. "I'm so sorry to hear it," he said, glancing at his watch, "but I'm afraid I have to run now." He began to edge away from her . . . "a bus to catch," he said.

"But wasn't that a legitimate use of summary dialogue?" Fred asks. "It was better than subjecting the reader to the whole boring monologue."

"Oh, sure! I didn't mean to imply one should never use it. But one shouldn't substitute it for speech when dialogue would serve one's purposes better. Sometimes beginning writers use summary dialogue to avoid having their characters talk."

Tension

"And there should be tension in the dialogue," Fred says, "as there was in the Ludlum and Steel passages. It seems to me that slack dialogue is probably about as boring as tons of exposition would be. Something ought to be happening between the people conversing."

"Dialogue ought always to be doing more than one thing," the Author types, nodding in agreement. "While it is going on it ought to be advancing the plot, or characterizing, or setting the scene, foreshadowing, or whatever, at the same time that it is operating as a medium for the exchange of information."

Again there is silence in the garret. The Author clears his throat but says nothing. He fidgets, staring at the monitor.

"Is that about it?" Fred asks at last.

"I guess that's it," the Author replies. "Did you learn anything else in our Socratic dialogue?"

"Several things, but one important question has been raised that hasn't been answered, it seems to me."

"As for instance?"

"Which of us is the Author, and which the foil?"

"You mean you think you're a real, not an invented character?"

"Maybe so."

"Why should you think that?"

"Because this is a book of *nonfiction* on the subject of dialogue."

"But it's also a book of *fiction* on a nonfiction subject."

"Not if I'm real," Fred Foyle points out.

"But you're not. However, you've been promoted."

"How's that?"

"I made you into a supporting character in an actual short story."

"Go on!"

"No, really, look":

The Museum of Ordinary People

They had been making these trips ever since their children had disappeared. Now, almost ten years later, they were on the road once more, driving through yet another little town they had never before seen. It was spring, the sun was warm. The pain had diminished over time until it was a dreary ache, but it was there, always. Every now and again it would put out a blossom of poison and then fade. It was the same for both of them.

"Look," Janet said, reaching over and touching Howard's hand as it rested on the steering wheel. She pointed through the windshield at a billboard.

"THE MUSEUM OF ORDINARY PEOPLE," Howard read aloud, "Five Miles Ahead on Route 12A." He blinked and frowned. His eyelids appeared to be paper thin, and the skin on his forehead not much thicker. One had the impression that the iris shone through, or the bone, but it was an illusion. His was a common sort of face.

So was Janet's. Both of them were beginning to gray, Howard more than his wife, but they were still on the farther edge of young adulthood. If they appeared to be older than they were, no doubt that was owing to their situation.

"Let's stop when we get there," Janet said. "We can take the time." She frowned also and covered her eyes briefly with her long fingers, then she smoothed her dress which was blue and wrinkling under the seat belt.

Howard braked suddenly and leaned across his wife to peer out the right window. "What is it?" Janet looked too—a boy and girl were playing in the front yard of a house with a moderate-sized lawn. He appeared to be about eleven and she, seven or so.

Janet sighed. "It can't be, Howard. You know that." She shook her head. "They're too young. When are you going to realize that?"

"Sorry," he said, sitting up straight and easing down on the accelerator. "Good thing there was nobody behind us." He glanced into the rear-view mirror as they moved slowly forward down the street of anonymous houses.

"They'd be ten years older," she said. "Billy would be a junior in college and Beth would be just out of high school."

"My mind knows that," Howard said, "but my guts don't."

They drove in silence for a few minutes, remembering the day the children hadn't come home from school.

There had been nothing unusual about it. All four of them had gotten up at seven in the morning, dressed, and had breakfast. "What are you going to do today?" Howard had asked the table at large.

Billy had shrugged and his pompadour had fallen down across his eyes. "Nothing much," he said, reaching for the butter. "We're having a spelling test is all."

"I think you need a haircut," Howard said to his son. "How about you?" He sent a droll wink in his daughter's direction and she giggled.

"Eat your cereal, Beth," Janet said. "You're just moving it around with your spoon. Don't you like it?"

"You put too much sugar in it."

"Okay, give it to me." Janet took the bowl over to the sink, poured some of the milk out of the cornflakes, which were beginning to look a little soggy, and added some fresh from the bottle on the counter.

"Okay, mom's fixed it," Howard said. "Now eat it up and let's go."

Beth began to scoop the cereal into her mouth. Billy got up and grabbed his backpack. "See you!" he yelled.

"Wait for your sister!" Janet said.

"Wait for me!" Beth squealed, grabbing her lunch box.

"Whoa!" Howard called as the front door slammed.

It opened again, briefly. "Bye!" Billy called and slammed it again.

And that was the last time anyone had ever seen either of the children.

"There's another one," Janet said, pointing ahead through the windshield.

THE MUSEUM OF ORDINARY PEOPLE, read the sign, *Three Miles Ahead. Largest Wax Museum in the Midwest.*

"How many do you suppose there are?" Janet asked.

"Not all that many, I wouldn't think." Howard had to bend to look as they passed.

They Move! They talk! The Experience of a Lifetime!
Don't Miss it!

A red light stopped them. "We need gas," Howard said.

"There's a place," Janet pointed again—it was a Seven-Eleven station up a half-block.

The light turned green and Howard pulled in and stopped at the pumps. "Fill it, please," he said to the attendant and got out of the car to stretch.

"Nice day," the attendant said as he unscrewed the gas cap and inserted the nozzle.

"Really nice." Howard put his hands on his hips and arched his back. The sun was warm on his face. "What's the name of this town?"

"Midville. Not from around here?" The pump hummed.

"Not so far away—a hundred miles or so. Lived here long?"

"All my life—twenty-one years." The tank was full, and the attendant rattled the nozzle against the rim and recapped it.

Howard reached into his pocket for his wallet, pulled out a bill and handed it over. His fingers hesitated, then he flipped to a picture of the children. He showed it to the young man. "Ever seen these two kids? They might have shown up in town when you were, oh, about eleven years old."

The attendant peered at the faces smiling out of the photograph. He hesitated, then he shook his head. "Can't say as I have," he said. He gave Howard a look as though he were going to ask a question but had decided against it.

Howard nodded. "Well, thanks." He took his change and put his wallet away. As he opened the door to get back into the car he said, "By the way, how's this Museum of Ordinary People up the road? Ever been there?"

"Oh, sure." The attendant turned to look up the street. "But not lately. Everybody's been there once, I guess. If you haven't, you ought to try it. It's good for a laugh." He nodded and turned to go back into the station. "Have a nice ride," he said.

Janet and Howard got back into the car and re-entered traffic. They were quiet for a few minutes. The trees along the curb were turning green quickly—it seemed almost as though spring had accelerated as they'd driven, but no doubt that was because the season was further along this far to the south. And then, as the houses began to grow sparser, the front yards to grow larger, and the trees to thicken, suddenly it was countryside and there were fields and few houses except at considerable distances.

Janet reached down and turned on the radio. She searched for a while and found a station they liked. For a few minutes they listened to golden oldies. And then they saw it. "There it is," Janet said.

Howard slowed down. "Are you sure?" he asked.

"Why not?" she said.

"'Admission $5.00,'" Howard said.

"Oh, I guess we can afford ten dollars, can't we?" Janet looked at her husband. "And it's not as though we're in a hurry," she added quietly, almost under her breath.

He smiled and nodded. "Sure we can." He pulled into the small parking lot and they sat in their seats for a moment or two listening to one of the old songs, then Howard turned off the motor.

When the children hadn't shown up by suppertime Janet and Howard had really begun to worry. They phoned around to the homes of schoolmates and friends and discovered that Beth and Billy hadn't been to school at all that day. The police had been notified then, and soon it was apparent that the kids had never even made it to their busses. They'd simply vanished between the house and the bus stop a block away.

The police canvassed the neighborhood, but no one remembered seeing the boy and girl in particular. Kids walking the streets in the morning were such a common sight that, even when someone thought he might have glimpsed the missing children, he wasn't sure it had been that particular day.

When at last Howard had been able to stop pacing or running to the door or driving around in the car peering out the windows into the shadows gathering and thickening among the houses of his neighbors, he joined his wife sitting next to the phone with a haunted stare in her eyes and a handkerchief in her fist. They had sat there like that all night long, waiting, jumping when the phone rang or the doorbell sounded, slumping when it turned out that there was no news. As the search went on neighbors and friends came and went with food and consolation, with assurances that Beth and Billy would turn up, that all would turn out well, that there would be a reasonable explanation for what had happened.

But they had been wrong, and a strange sort of emptiness began to occupy Janet and Howard from that point onward. The rooms of their dwelling filled with a silence that cried out for quick movement and loud music. A veil of anxiety settled itself between the parents and their home—nothing seemed to be real, to be solid or stable, not even their marriage, although they drew closer together after an initial repulsion, like magnets reversed, for each wanted at first to blame the other for what had happened. Common sense had prevailed, however; they saw that nothing could have been done to prevent the loss of Billy and Beth, for it could not have been foreseen.

When at last the police had no leads left to follow, when the story faded from the back pages of the newspapers, when even a private investigator could offer no more hope, on the weekends and on their vacations Howard and Janet would drive in any direction, show their pictures, ask their questions.

"Are we going in?" Janet asked.

Howard roused himself and shivered a little. "Oh, sure, hon," he said and got out. By the time he'd walked around the car Janet had gotten out herself and stood waiting. Together, they walked to the door of the museum and went in.

It was a large old Victorian house. Just inside the door, in a wide hallway, there stood an oak table where an old woman sat selling tickets. "Welcome to the Museum of Ordinary People," she said nodding mechanically and leaning forward. "That will be five dollars apiece." Howard gave her the money. She opened a drawer in the table, deposited it inside, and handed him two tickets. "Please take a brochure," she said in her odd monotone. "It will explain the museum. Please walk straight ahead." She sat back, blinked her eyes slowly, and said no more.

As they walked down the corridor toward the first door Janet leaned close to Howard and whispered, "Doesn't she remind you of someone?"

Howard paused, glanced over his shoulder, frowned, and said, "You're right, but I can't think who."

"Let's look at the brochure," Janet said.

The museum of ordinary people is a unique exhibit, it began, in that there is nothing extraordinary about it except its premise. Here the visitor will find the people he knows saying the things he would expect them to say. The waxwork figures are completely lifelike, even to their movements, for they are animated by extremely sophisticated electronic components which are capable of smoothly imitating natural muscle action. The recorded voices are those of real people responding to real situations and dialogue. Please enter and enjoy yourself in an imitation of the real world that is so convincing as to be astonishing. If the exhibit is successful, it will make reality seem fresh and new—it will give you a new perspective on your own life.

Howard looked at Janet with eyebrows arched high on his papery forehead. She stared back at him, the phantom of a smile playing across her mouth. "Well," he said, "let's give it a try. I'm willing to be amazed."

"It sounds like fun."

He opened the door and they entered.

"Well, hello there!" said a woman on the other side. "It's real nice to see you, hon," she said. She had on a waitress' uniform; there was a pencil stuck behind her ear and a sales pad slipped through her belt. "Geez, when was the last time you was in here? Musta been a long time."

"We've never been here before," Janet said. "We didn't realize this was a restaurant too."

"Oh, never mind, just let me tell ya what's good today. The soup's good—minestrone they call it, but it's just vegetable soup. And then our specials . . ."

"Thanks," Howard said, "But we're not hungry. We'll just look at the rest of the exhibits." He smiled politely, his hand gentle but firm on Janet's back as they moved past.

". . . are liver 'n onions with bacon, chicken fried steak. . . ." and then she stopped talking and stood still, facing toward the door.

"Look, Howard," Janet said nodding toward a beam of light through which they had stepped. "She's one of the wax figures."

"We tripped an electric eye," Howard said sticking his finger into the ray. "Unbelievable."

"Well, sir," an elderly male voice said behind them, "that was back in 'sixty-six as I recall, and I never caught a better fish since." They turned quickly and saw the replica of a dock with a boathouse where an old man sat leaning forward in his rocking chair whittling a piece of wood. "Sure would like to run into a fighter like that big-mouth again." He nodded and chuckled.

"Straight out of my childhood," Howard said. "That looks just like the boatkeeper at Huntington Lake."

Janet laughed uneasily. "I feel like telling you to be quiet because he'll hear you," she said. "They really are lifelike." She walked on.

"Sorry, folks," the policeman said. He stood with his hands behind him and shook his head. "There's been an accident down this street and you'll have to keep clear. The fire department's laying down some foam over the spilled gasoline." He pointed with his nightstick. "It's not much farther if you go that way."

"Thank you, officer," Janet said before she could catch herself.

Howard grinned. "Probably the accident's in the living room," he said. Janet laughed and flushed.

They lost track of time. Every room held a crowd of ordinary people who spoke to them, offered advice, asked directions, complained—like the fat woman on the mock-up of a bus who said, "Oh, my feet ache. I been on my tootsies all day long, and now I gotta go home and make supper for my old man. Will he appreciate it? Oh, no," she said shaking her head, making her chins wiggle and her red hair with the brown roots jounce, "he'll just sit there after supper with a beer watching Monday Night Football while I do the dishes." She snorted. "Boy, I could do with a beer myself, come to think of it."

And there was the journalist sitting at his word-processor typing a story. "Fred Foyle," he said, turning around as they entered his office. "What can I do for you?" He had a thin face and a shock of pale hair that fell down over his eye. "Want ads? That's over there at the classified desk," he said pointing. "Can't help you." He turned back to his screen. Janet and Howard heard him sigh. "Obits!" he snorted. "This week I'm on obits. Next week I'll be on garden parties." He hunched forward and began to type, still mumbling.

"I'm starting to get hungry," Howard said. They were standing in an upstairs hallway looking out a bay window over the countryside. The sun was beginning to settle into the fields and appearing redder as it did so. There was a wind, too, that could be seen but not heard, riffling through the few trees visible in the landscape.

"That was a lot of fun," Janet said. "It was like walking through a whole town full of people that you feel you know."

"I wonder who got the idea for such a museum." Howard mused a moment and then said, "well, I guess that's about it. What say we hunt up some food and then head home?" A gust of wind rattled the window behind them as they turned toward the stairway. "Too bad that waitress downstairs isn't real."

"Oh, look," Janet said, "there's a doorway we missed." She walked across the carpet and paused with her hand on the knob of a door that looked out of place in the old Victorian building. Out of place but familiar, like almost everything else in the Museum of Ordinary People.

"Never mind it," Howard said. "I've seen enough, haven't you?"

"Oh, let's just have a peek," Janet replied, and before her husband could reply she turned the knob and pulled open the door. The house exhaled as they stood looking between the jambs.

"It's the attic stairway," Howard said peering upward into the gloom over Janet's shoulder.

She put her foot on the first stair. "Shall we go up?" she asked even as she shifted her weight forward. "There may be more exhibits."

"There doesn't seem to be a light switch." But he followed her. In a moment they were standing at the top of the flight listening to the hum of a wasp on the ceiling and the sound of a lawnmower in the hands of a distant neighbor. They stood quietly for a few moments peering into the shadows. They could make out a clothes rack filled with outmoded fashions, trunks and boxes. There was a film of dust lying upon everything.

A god's-eye stood raveling colored yarn beneath the narrow garret window. A girl's ballerina slipper lay beside it. A box of toys contained Pinocchio with a rubber nose. Winter lay preserved in a carton of Christmas tree ornaments, but the musty odors of summer sweltered in the nooks and cracks between objects. An umbrella waited for the sound of rain to come drumming over the roof.

"It's late," Howard said. "I'm hungry." He smiled. "I've had enough, haven't you?"

Janet hesitated, then she smiled back at him and let her hand fold into his, but before they could turn and descend the stairs out of the dim place where time lay in keeping, they heard the door close behind them.

"That's the character you made me into?" Fred stares fixedly at the Author. "You made me into a bit player? A robot journalist?"

"Well, it's a step up, isn't it? It's almost as good as being real, no?"

"No! Nowhere near as good. What makes you think you're real?" Fred asks.

"I had the first word in the book, the genesis, as it were, so I'm the prime cause of this treatise."

"You may have had the first word," Fred Foyle points out, "but I'll have the last one."

(Acknowledgments continued from page iv)

"One Sunday Morning," appeared in *The Carleton Miscellany,* x:3, Summer 1969. "Pleasant Dell" was also published in *The Carleton Miscellany,* vi:2, Spring 1965. Both are here reprinted by permission of the author.

"Pocoangelini 7" is from *Pocoangelini: A Fantography and Other Poems,* Northampton: Despa Press, 1971, and is reprinted here by permission of the author. © 1971, 2004 by Lewis Turco, all rights reserved.

"Savants" is from *Sucarnochee Review,* Vol. vi, 1988 and is reprinted here by permission of the author. © 1989, 2004 by Lewis Turco, all rights reserved.

"Scot on the Rocks" originally appeared in *The Miscellany* (subsequently *The Davidson Miscellany*), iv: 1, January 1969, and is reprinted here by permission of the author. © 1969, 1989, 2004 by Lewis Turco, all rights reserved.

"Shipmates" appeared first in *Colorado-North Review,* xv:3, Spring 1978 and is reprinted here by permission of the author. © 1978, 2004 by Lewis Turco, all rights reserved.

Index

Page numbers in **bold** indicate defined terms in the text. Page numbers in *italics* indicate extracted or complete quoted texts.